Hello, my name is Matt and I've got a confession to make. I'm a running addict! There, I feel better now. I just thought I had better share this with you before I tell you my plans to make you:

a runner...
a better runner...
and a *happy* runner

I can't say that running changed my life because, actually, it completely shaped it. I grew up around sport and carried on to compete and to train with the world's leading athletes. Through my teenage years I trained as a sprinter to a high level in ways that were exhilarating, exhausting, torturous and revealing. It is the point in my life at which I can honestly say I discovered just how far a body can be pushed! Since then various sports have featured in my life at different times but it is always running I return to. It is always challenging and always rewarding.

When I tell people my story about my own sporting experiences, there is a natural assumption that I must be able to run long distances like half marathons and marathons without even breaking sweat. Yet nothing could be further from the truth!

As a genetic body type that is predisposed to sprint and power tests, I am least enabled to do long, endurance-type events. In fact, while I was training as a sprinter it was exceptionally rare for me to run any further than around 600 metres in anything other than a very slow warm-up jog!

So, for me, personally, getting into running long distances was always a real challenge as I battled against what I was made to do, and what I had then subsequently trained to do even more specifically. The point of this aside? We *all* face challenges in running and we *all* have little battles to win, but the real beauty of running and the amazing thing about our bodies is that they adapt when needed to the new demands. It isn't always easy, but it is always possible and is *always* incredibly rewarding.

These days I work with runners of all abilities all of the time and they all have to be guided and pushed through appropriate routines for their needs – overcoming a range of different barriers along the way. Though running is a relatively simple thing, to give yourself the best chance of really achieving something (and most importantly really enjoying it) there's quite a lot you need to know.

In this book I will take you through everything that you need to know about running. What you should wear on your body and on your feet, and why. What you need to eat, when you need to eat it and what it does for you. How you warm up, cool down, stretch, mobilise, hydrate and focus your mind – there are many different areas to address. Some of these will be things you didn't know but wanted to find out about; others will be things that you didn't know that you didn't know, but will change how you run forever!

You may be thinking about starting running to get healthier or lose weight. You may be thinking about running because you want to get fit fast, or you may already be a runner, but thinking about taking the next step and trying a race. Whatever your level, this book will provide you with everything you need to know about how to run well while also giving you a number of programmes for reaching various distance goals. I have also included a number of strength training programmes that will optimise your performance as well as some incredible track sessions to vary your programme, test your body and make you quicker and stronger. In running, there are often little niggles, aches and minor strains along the way, particularly as you increase distances. There is a whole section in this book that guides you through dealing with these and makes sure that your chances of getting them in the first place are minimised.

Personally, I have run 5K, 10K, half marathon and marathon events at fast paces even though my body isn't ideally suited to these distances. The plans that you'll find in this book are the ones that I use on myself and with my clients all of the time. They are simple, easy to follow and, most importantly, they work!

This book is designed to give you all the support, advice, information and focus necessary to make your route to success as clear as possible. While the hard work is down to you, the training and preparation advice contained within these pages will, hopefully, give you that little push to help you on the way and to get you feeling the same way about running as I do.

My name is Matt, I am a running addict and, once you've finished this book, you will be too!

GETTING
STARTED

WHY RUN?

In my opinion running is the single most rewarding and beneficial form of exercise that there is.

Running is powerful! It is the most accessible form of exercise and can be done in pretty much any environment, at any time and by anybody. We are born, developed and destined to run. You only have to watch a child for a few moments to understand our natural instinct to run – put a group of children into any sort of space and it won't be long before there is some running involved. We run for fun, we run for the bus and we run to compete and win. Running impacts on many, many parts of our lives and we go back for more all of the time.

It is often said that what makes runners run is that quest for the "runner's high" – that fabled rush of adrenaline that reaching a level of running ability, confidence and contentment brings and which makes all of the hard work worthwhile. The truth is that running has many highs (and many lows too, at times) but it never ceases to allow you to explore, push and discover new levels of ability, satisfaction and utter self-satisfaction.

ENJOY THE JOURNEY

If you ask any regular runner what their favourite running route is, I can guarantee that each and every one of them will not only be able to tell you exactly where it is, but also to explain to you in some detail why they love it so much and what it does to them physically in terms of a challenge.

One of the things that I like to do whenever I travel is to go for a run as soon as possible when I reach my destination. I use it as my way of getting to know my territory. When I reach a new city, I like to explore it first by running to get my bearings before going back later to take more time. When I go to somewhere more rural, I like to go and find out what the terrain and countryside is really like by finding the best and most testing trails I can, and ideally finding the best views of the area as I do so. I am not a walker! I am happier to explore an area at speed by running than to cover a fraction of the distance while walking. Indeed a number of decisions I have taken on matters like where to live, holiday and travel have in no small part been influenced by the possibilities of where I will run. Obsessive? Actually, no. Satisfied and fulfilled by good running? Absolutely.

NEW TO RUNNING?

Of course if you are not a regular runner, or you are coming at it having not really run for some considerable time, all talk of favourite routes, reaching highs, being empowered and finding out how good you can feel will sound really alien to you. In fact, just running up and down your garden might seem like a journey into the unknown. Don't worry, you are very far from alone!

If you are new to running, you are about to enter a whole new experience of physical accomplishment. You must start slowly. One of the biggest mistakes that any overly enthusiastic newcomer can make is to run too far or too fast too soon, and then suffer the aches, strains and pains that demotivate and disrupt the whole process of getting started.

HOW FAR SHOULD I RUN TO START OFF WITH?

In many ways, starting off is one of the best parts of running – it's a time where you can take it easy while experiencing some really rapid development. Like weight-loss, the hardest part is often that last bit when you are getting close to your goal. As you progressively increase your distances over a period of weeks (not days), your body very quickly adapts and enables you to run further and faster than you might have imagined was possible. As you make progress and you reach set targets you will begin to feel the changes in mentality and physicality that are behind the so-called "runner's high" – that elusive combination of achieving a new target or level, the chemical release of endorphins (nature's "feel-good drug") into your body, the sensation of running itself and a vast array of other personal experiences all of which join together to leave you in a state of satisfied well-being.

And there you see how quickly we go from starting slowly to feeling great. I, like any other passionate runner, can't help but extol the virtues of the thing that I love to do the most, but it *will* be you too, and sooner than you think.

A BRIEF HISTORY OF MODERN RUNNING

Running is as old as mankind. Whether to kill our dinner, avoid being eaten, rage battles with foreign armies, compete in events and games or simply to just get a bit fitter and lose some weight, we have always been runners.

In modern times, however, it has only really been since the 1960s and '70s that running became the popular choice for recreational fitness that it is now. New Zealand-based coach Arthur Lydiard is perhaps most credited for this kickstart in running's popularity. Widely acknowledged as the man responsible for coining the term "jogging" in 1962, he was in the vanguard of a number of other coaches and athletes, such as Bill Bowerman and Jim Fixx, who wrote articles and books which helped build running's understanding and appeal.

Four decades later and running is now the most popular sport in the world. Go to any city in the Western world and you'll find a large number of running competitions for all levels, distances and terrains. As an example of its popularity, the London Marathon hosts approximately 35,000 runners every year, but receives more than four times that number of applications. Marquee marathons like New York, Chicago, Paris and Berlin all tell the same story – we love to run!

But why is running so popular? Well, aside from being able to provide a great competitive fix, running is the quickest, simplest solution for getting fitter and leaner. It also involves little or no cost to perform. In fact, through race sponsorship it is now one of the biggest raisers of charity funds in the world, and it is this ability to raise money for good causes that holds running's appeal for many. Its popularity now is such that I bet you know at least one person who has run in an organised running event.

But where is running heading? As we've become accustomed to the running of half marathon and marathon distances as "normal", certain people have pushed endurance events to a whole new level. Now every year runners line up for some of the most extreme tests of human endurance: events such as the Marathon De Sables, the Spartathlon and Badwater Death Valley (see right). Runners are continually extending boundaries as they strive to go further and faster.

ULTRA-DISTANCE EVENTS

The **MARATHON DE SABLES** is a six-day, 151-mile running competition that takes place in the Moroccan Sahara sands in heats of up to 42°C. Carrying their own supplies of food and water on their backs, competitors run from point to point every day and battle to overcome the heat, energy depletion and poor terrain to reach their monumental target.

If that doesn't sound hard enough for you, why not try the **SPARTATHLON**? This non-stop 152-mile run between the Acropolis in Athens to Sparta, retracing the supposed journey of the Greek messenger after the Battle of Marathon (after which the marathon distance is now named), takes a staggering 25–35 hours to complete. Only half of the entrants ever make the finishing line, with the rest being eliminated at time checks along the way.

Still not tough enough for you? Only real ultra-distance afficionados should consider the **BADWATER ULTRAMARATHON**, which must be the toughest of them all. This 135-mile non-stop run takes place in the infamous Death Valley in California's Mojave Desert. If you catch a hot day the temperature can reach a searing 55°C. As a result this race represents the very outer limit of our ability to run.

GET RUNNING FAST

This book contains all you need to help get you up and off your sofa and out running. In here you'll find everything you need to know about training, technique, equipment and diet, along with a whole host of tips and insights that will help give you that little extra edge. To help you navigate the information, I've worked up a fast track for those of you who can't wait to get up and running straight away. Use it to get yourself going as quickly as possible.

GET READY

ASSESS YOUR RUNNING STYLE AND GAIT by reading about the mechanics of running on pages 20–25 and taking the tests on page 26–33 to establish which areas you need to work on.

KIT YOURSELF UP with the appropriate equipment after reading through the gear section on pages 42–46, paying particular attention to footwear.

GET SET

SET YOUR GOAL by selecting a distance you want to achieve from the programme section on pages 78–155. This section contains detailed programmes for distances from 5K to ultra distance and for all running abilities, so there should be something here for everyone.

GO!

FOLLOW YOUR CHOSEN PROGRAMME IN FULL remembering that all elements of the programme are important. Don't *just* complete the running and forget about the resistance elements of the programme, as these will increase your power and efficiency.

REMEMBER TO WARM UP AND COOL DOWN thoroughly before every training session, following the stretching and mobility routines given on pages 52–61. If you find that you are suffering from any injuries, check the section on pages 66–73 for advice.

STRUGGLING FOR MOTIVATION? If you're finding things difficult and need a little help to keep you going, turn to pages 40–41 for tips on how to get over the training blues.

WHAT'S YOUR AEROBIC ENDURANCE?

Your aerobic endurance is a reflection of how
easily your body can take on oxygen and
utilise it when required. Test your aerobic
endurance by running for a mile on a treadmill
and recording your time. If you prefer, measure
your distance outside over one mile and time
yourself there. If your treadmill only has
kilometres, then time yourself over 1.6K.

Level 1	*12 mins*
Level 2	*10 mins*
Level 3	*9 mins*
Level 4	*8 mins*
Level 5	*7 mins*

Retest yourself every few weeks – aiming to
reach the higher levels – once you've started
one of the training programmes detailed on
pages 78–155.

THE PHYSIOLOGY OF RUNNING

While there's no one single exercise that covers all facets of fitness, running comes close. As with pretty much all exercise, the extent to which running works your body depends upon your level of intensity. Running is highly adaptable and allows a great range of different intensities to be reached depending on how you do it.

At one end of the scale is **sprinting** – a power-based approach that encourages and stimulates significant strengthening of the leg, torso and core muscles (and to a lesser extent the upper body) while also providing an enormous stimulus to the metabolism and to the strength of the cardio-respiratory system. When sprinters train, they use short periods of running, perhaps between 5 and 90 seconds, at an intensity that is always pushing close to the very upper-end of performance levels, with relatively long recovery periods in which to allow the body to recover before the next bout of high-intensity effort begins. The intensity of a sprint and the workload required by the muscles to propel your body forwards can be likened to the experience of lifting weights, in that your body is completing a relatively small number of movements (or repetitions) at a high resistance, which in turn forces it to adapt and grow muscle. At the same time, this high-intensity effort has a profound effect on the metabolism of the body and increases enormously the amount of calories required to sustain the body.

At the other end of the scale is **endurance-based running** over distances such as 10K, half marathon and marathon length – the sort of running that this book is primarily concerned with. Endurance-based running is of a much lower level of intensity than sprinting, is carried out with little or no rest or recovery within running sessions and is sustained for a much longer duration. The effect of such an effort is to place more pressure on your cardiovascular system, your heart and lungs, to keep you moving. This slower, lower-intensity effort is carried out "aerobically" (with oxygen), in marked contrast to sprinting, which does not rely upon oxygen and is "anaerobic", instead relying on energy sources which are found within the body already. Aerobic training is very effective at increasing the functioning capacity of the lungs, the heart and the capillary system to cope with the oxygen and blood demands around the body.

Between these two extremes there is everything else! 5K runs, football, tennis, rugby, trail running, fell running – they all involve running, but in ways that test the body differently and require a completely different set of skills and training to perfect. This wide variety of different uses just proves how important running is to all of us, and how making the most of your training helps to increase your ability to perform when required to.

WHAT DOES RUNNING DO TO YOUR BODY?

Running affects the way our bodies work down to a cellular level. The benefits of embarking on a regular training programme not only for performance reasons but also from a health perspective are incredibly well documented.

A STRONGER HEART

Running can have a profoundly positive effect on the whole of your body, starting with the most important muscle of all – your heart. The heart is responsible for taking oxygen from the lungs and delivering it to the muscles via the blood passing through your body's arterial/capillary network. Regular running will result in the enlargement and strengthening of the heart muscle, which improves the ability to pump blood around the body, as well as an improved coronary blood supply (blood supply to the heart). In older individuals with concerns about their heart health, regular training can reduce the risk of heart attack, lower their resting heart rate and protect them from elevated blood pressure complications. The improvements in efficiency of the heart lower the heart rate needed to perform a given workload, in turn reducing stress on the heart and reducing the risk factors of a cardio-respiratory incident.

Running (as with all regular, vigorous aerobic exercise) also improves heart health by improving blood cholesterol levels – increasing the number of beneficial high-density lipoproteins, while reducing the number of harmful low-density lipoproteins. Lower harmful cholesterol generally results in decreased arterial blood pressure, meaning a reduction in the tendency of blood clots and other heart-related complications. These factors (which are also diet-related) highlight the way in which regular running can have a profoundly positive effect on the whole of the body.

TRAINING VS EXERCISE

I need to stress that, when I refer to "training" in this book, I have in mind something very different from the simple performing of "exercise". The aim of training is to get better at something over time in response to regular challenges. With running, this improvement comes as a result of the body's ability to adapt quickly both in the way that it uses energy and by improving its neural (nerve) and muscular efficiency.

INCREASED CARDIOVASCULAR FITNESS

A distance runner needs oxygenated blood to be delivered at a constant pace over an extended period of time, without any undue strain. Regular training causes an increase of blood plasma volume and an increase in the total number of red blood cells – improving oxygen transport and resulting in a more effective exchange process at the lungs. This is vital not only for getting oxygen into the body, but also for transporting waste products from exercise to the lungs and kidneys for removal from the body.

There are also a number of benefits that running brings which further improve the body's ability to process oxygen and get rid of waste products. Lung ventilation is improved by the strengthening of respiratory muscles, while improved blood supply results in an improvement in the lungs' ability to extract oxygen from the air that has been inhaled.

STRUCTURAL IMPROVEMENTS AT CELL LEVEL AND BEYOND

At a cellular level, changes can be seen in the way that longer-distance running can improve and enhance energy utilisation. This can also be seen in cell structure, where running leads to an increase in the size and density of mitochondria – the cell's energy powerhouses which are more prevalent in slow-twitch muscle fibres. In relation to endurance-based events, increasing the volume of mitochondria improves exercise efficiency as it means there are more sites to process energy quickly. Mitochondria numbers improve over time with regular aerobic exercise.

Beyond cell level, there are positive structural changes all over the body. Regular aerobic exercise can cause thickening of articular cartilage and bones, improving the body's ability to tolerate load and enabling it to move more effectively with minimal injury. In an untrained individual, regular running will also develop lean muscle tissue, which will enhance metabolic rate and improve the body's structural strength.

RUNNING OFF THE BLUES
In addition to the physiological benefits covered here, running has a number of proven psychological benefits including the improvement of mental alertness; reduction of depression and anxiety; an improvement in the ability to relax (which should lead to better quality of sleep) as well as improvements in stress tolerance.

HARDER-WORKING MUSCLES

Your muscles' main sources of fuel are glycogen (carbohydrate) and fat, which they break down into the energy they need in order to work. With regular training your body becomes more efficient at using less of this glycogen for a given workload. This is termed glycogen sparing and is often responsible for the "plateau" effect – when someone who is undertaking an exercise regime feels that the progress they are making has come to a halt as the body has adapted to utilise less energy to perform the same movement. Thankfully, we can get around this by switching up our training (by varying its intensity, volume or amount) as the programmes on pages 78–155 demonstrate.

This is not the only change that running brings to your body's energy usage; as the intensity of your running increases, your muscles will be working harder and will need to metabolise fat at a faster rate. Effectively, we become more efficient fat burners with more exercise (it does take time to improve this efficiency, however). If you carry too much body fat, you may not be an efficient fat burner, but with training this can improve, enhancing your metabolism and improving not only your performance but also your health.

INCREASED STAMINA

Fatigue is often cited as the factor that most hampers a person's enjoyment of exercise, and it is often caused by the burning sensation within the muscles that intense exercise can bring. This sensation is due to a build-up of lactic acid – a by-product of converting glucose into energy – within the muscles. The build-up occurs when the body crosses what is termed the "lactate threshold", the point at which, because so much energy has been used in a short space of time, more lactic acid has been produced than can be pumped away, with the effect that your performance will be affected. Thankfully, a lifting of the ability to process lactic acid – and therefore a raising of the body's lactate threshold – is one of the benefits of regular training. Working at or around your lactate threshold pace can help develop the efficiency of the body to clear this acidic state and will help maintain your exercise intensity.

MORE EFFICIENT MUSCLES

Over a period of training, as with any exercise, the efficiency of the movement itself – the way in which the muscles are working together – will improve. Training with correct running style is important as it improves muscle functioning and protects the body against over-use injury. Developing full-body intramuscular coordination is important in running and, with some of my trainees, I suggest a period of strength training before launching into a full running programme. Too many runners have their progress hampered by lack of stability and strength, from a muscle-functioning perspective. Indeed, if you have any injuries, aches or pains in the knees, lower back or neck, I suggest you get checked out by a qualified professional before you begin running.

THE MECHANICS OF RUNNING

Every year there is a great deal written about the best way to run, with many different people telling us that their particular running style is the best and only way to do so.

The most common styles discussed are barefoot running, heel-strike running, mid-foot running and forefoot running (see box opposite for details). Each one of these running styles, depending on who you listen to, supposedly offers the most efficient, most comfortable or most injury-free running. But which one is correct?

The answer, to some degree, is that *any* of these may be correct for an individual, as running is more about the person doing it than the technique itself.

Barefoot (and to a lesser extent forefoot) runners put forward the argument that we humans were never designed to run on our heels and that we should therefore run in the same style as our ancestors and those tribal groups around the globe who still run barefoot. The examples they frequently give are the Maasai warriors of Kenya and the Tarahumara Indians of Mexico.

To a certain extent, they are right – people are designed to hit the ground, when running naturally towards the front of their feet. Interestingly, if you ask someone to run barefoot, nine times out of ten that person will automatically move to running on the front of the foot. This is because it is actually pretty painful to land on an unprotected heel! At the Matt Roberts Running Clinic we perform hundreds of biomechanics assessments on runners every year and no matter how much of a heel-strike runner someone is in trainers, when you ask them to run on the treadmill barefoot they will tend to change their style.

This, however, does not mean that forefoot running is correct for everyone who wants to run. From all the analysis that we have done and all the research that we have undertaken there is only one certainty – that the human body has been designed to run, full stop. Although it is undeniable that the anatomical position of the heel is not conducive to being landed on, modern running shoes with good support and cushioning in the heel area do allow us to run in this way effectively.

The physically stronger you are, the better the condition of your muscles and the less sedentary your lifestyle, the more likely you are to be able to cope with and benefit from running towards the front of your foot. The weaker and tighter the muscles of your body and the more sedentary your lifestyle, the less likely you will be able to cope with front-foot running. That is not to say that you will never be ready for it, but running style is something that is progressive.

Distance and speed of running also affect running action. A shorter, faster distance run needs to be powered by a more explosive running action – every foot strike needs to propel the runner forward, while the muscles of the calves, quadriceps, hamstrings and glutes all need to be strong enough to work hard over a short distance. A long-distance run, by contrast, is about efficiency and holding off the

RUNNING STYLES

HEEL-STRIKE RUNNING
Heel-strike runners hit the ground with their heels and roll through to push-off. Runners who heel-strike need to pay more attention to the support and cushioning offered by their trainers.

MID-FOOT/FOREFOOT RUNNING
Mid-foot/forefoot strikers rarely touch the ground with their heels, especially when running fast, and have shorter ground contact time.

BAREFOOT RUNNING
Barefoot runners hit the ground with the lateral edge of the forefoot. Proponents of barefoot running argue that it is healthier for feet and reduces the risk of chronic injuries, notably repetitive stress injuries due to the impact of heel striking in padded running shoes.

effects of fatigue and muscular wear and tear. As a result, you will never use the same running action for a 400m run as you do to run a marathon – the actions are different because of the different requirements of each task and the different requirements of power and efficiency.

Bearing all this in mind, to work out the best running style for any individual we have to consider:

A) the running experience of the individual
B) the muscular strength of the individual
C) the mobility and flexibility of the individual
D) the running goal of the individual

As you can see, it is impossible for one running action to fit everyone because, by the time you analyse all the above criteria, very few of us will come out needing the same things.

RUNNING GAIT

Running gait refers to the style in which you run and the applied forces on the body as you move forward. While you are most likely to come across this term when you are buying a pair of running shoes – where you are assessed for the way in which your foot strikes the floor and therefore which type of shoe best suits your needs – your running "gait" actually refers to how you carry your *whole body* through movement and the relationship between all your bones, joints and muscles.

If you observe a number of the great runners in action, you will not see the same posture, style, stride length or foot strike in all of them. However, what you will see is efficient, effortless forward momentum and an ability to cover distance with what appears to be graceful ease. This is the lesson we have to learn as a runner, not that we all have to conform to one technique for fear of injury or incorrectness. We have to accept that there are different styles of running to suit different people before finding the style that works best for each of us individually. Finally, we have to work on perfecting that style while working on our weaknesses.

THERE IS NO SUCH THING AS "CORRECT" RUNNING STYLE

Every style of running can be wrong. We see injuries in our clinics every day that have been caused because someone has changed to barefoot running, or has chosen to work on adopting a mid-foot running style because a running friend said they should. Likewise, we see major foot tendon problems because someone is heavy on their feet and they heel-strike too harshly. It is easy to be convinced by a convert to a running style that you should do it too. However, the best thing to do is to assess your style first (using the advice and tests outlined on the following pages). Only after doing this should you even *consider* whether there is a good reason to change.

With the exception of actual barefoot running, which is quite simply impractical and dangerous, each of the running styles has its own place and can be effective. For example, I have seen and heard of great achievements in injury prevention and running improvements from people switching from heel-striking to mid-foot running, from those learning to run mid-foot to forefoot with the use of minimalist running shoes, and from those learning to run heel-strike but with fast foot action and heel pick up. I regularly see big improvements in people who have used barefoot running shoes to help strengthen their feet by doing drills on grass. Remember too that you don't have to decide to fix your running in one style – mixing up styles of running also works very well as it stops the foot from getting too used to running in a certain way.

RUNNING DON'TS

Whatever running style you choose, there are some things you should try to steer clear of doing . The following common problems among runners can affect performance in terms of both speed and endurance and can contribute to injury as they place additional strain on various parts of the body.

Lordosis
Over-extension in the lower back results in this "duck-like" posture. It can be corrected by stretching of the hip flexors and hamstrings.

Crouched-over posture
This common position inhibits stride length and may build pressure in the upper back and neck joints. It can be corrected by strengthening the upper and middle back and increasing mobility through the shoulders and chest.

Lateral hip movement
The outwards push of the pelvis here, caused by poor strength in the lower back, glutes and adominals, results in lower back pain and hip joint damage. This can be corrected by improving core strength.

Medial knee roll
This inwards roll of the knee, which causes damage to the medial ligaments and cartilage of the knee capsule, can be corrected by strengthening the quads and increasing flexibility in the hamstrings and adductors.

Flutter kick
This unstable posture, which results in excessive strain to the hip, knee and lower back joints, can be corrected by strengthening the glutes and hips, and increasing flexibility in the ITBs.

RUNNING DO'S

Whatever style you opt for there are some key factors that you should always look for in your running style:

• Make sure that when you pick your heel up off the ground you focus on using the buttock muscles to pull the leg through and then the hamstrings to pick the heel up.

• Remember that faster, shorter strides are better than slow long ones.

• Keep bouncing to a minimum – running is about floating over the ground not bouncing along it on heavy feet.

• Keep tall through the torso so that your core muscles work to both drive the body forward and to help you breath easier as the rib cage is not squashed.

• Make sure that you are not running too upright and tucking your bottom under as this will put stress the base and top of your spine.

• Aim to bring your heel on your trailing leg up to knee level as you run.

• Land softly on your feet, not heavily and rolling hard through the foot.

ASSESSING YOUR RUNNING STYLE

To look at improving your individual running style, the first thing you need to do is to map out the strengths and weaknesses of your body. The series of self-tests outlined here will help you work out your individual training requirements. Once you've completed the tests, check the Conclusions to Tests on page 33 to see which areas you need to improve on and how to go about doing so.

CORE TEST
Using the muscles of the abdominals, hold both the plank position and the oblique plank positions as illustrated (see pages 176–177 for detailed descriptions), for as long as you can.

RESULTS: PLANK
• **30–60 secs** (poor)
• **60–90 secs** (average)
• **90+ secs** (good)

SIDE PLANK
• **30–45 secs** (poor)
• **45–60 secs** (average)
• **60+ secs** (good)

SINGLE LEG TEST

Start seated on a chair that is about knee high. Lift one leg off the floor, then try to come up to a standing position with the use of just the one leg.

RESULTS:
- **Inability to get up indicates poor glute strength and/or poor quad or lower back strength.**

HAMSTRING TEST

Lying flat on your back on the floor, lift one leg up straight as far as your can, keeping the other leg on the floor. Note the approximate degree to which you have raised your leg from the horizontal. Lower and repeat with the other leg.

RESULTS:
- **Below 70°** (very poor)
- **70–80°** (poor)
- **80–90°** (good)
- **Over 90°** (very good)

HIP FLEXOR TEST

Lying flat on your back, bring both legs in towards your body as tight as you can. Now, holding one leg in to your chest as tight as you can, allow the other leg to stretch back out towards the floor as far as it can.

RESULTS:
• **Leg cannot keep straight and reach floor** (very poor)
• **Foot touching ground but knee of held leg cannot reach chest** (poor)
• **Foot on ground but back of knee and most of calf muscle raised off floor** (below average)
• **Leg down with all of calf touching the ground and other knee still tight into chest** (good)

LOWER BACK TEST

Lying on your back on the floor, bring both knees in towards your chest as close as you can.

RESULTS:
• **Knees cannot reach chest** (poor)
• **Knees come into chest with effort** (average)
• **Knees come into chest easily** (good)

UPPER BACK TEST

Stand with your heels, buttocks and shoulder blades against a wall. Maintain a small curve in the lower back and take your elbows up so that your elbows and hands are touching the wall out to the side of the body. Once in this position move the arms up above the head, aiming to keep the hands and elbows in contact with the wall at all times.

RESULTS:
- **Unable to get elbows and hands to touch the wall in start position** (very poor)
- **Elbows come away from wall once above shoulder height** (poor)
- **Only fingers touch wall at top end of movement** (average)
- **Elbows and hands touch wall throughout movement** (good)

CALF/ACHILLES TEST

Stand with both feet together about a quarter-foot away from a wall. Keeping the feet flat on the floor, push the knees towards the wall without tilting the pelvis. If the knees touch the wall without the heels lifting, move back and repeat.

RESULTS:
- **Heels lift a quarter-foot length from wall** (below average)
- **Heels lift a half-foot length away from the wall** (average)
- **Heels lift more than a half-foot length away from the wall** (good)

CHEST TEST

Lie on your side with your knees bent up at 45° and your shoulders at 90° to the floor. Take your arms straight out in front of you at shoulder level. Keeping your shoulders at 90° to the floor, take your top arm back as far as you can while looking forward at all times. Note the approximate degree to which you have taken your arm back from the horizontal.

RESULTS:
- **Up to 120°** (poor)
- **120–160°** (average)
- **160–180°** (good)

HIP TEST

Lie on your side with your knees bent up at 45° and hips and shoulders at 90°. From this position, lift your top leg up as far as you can without allowing the hips to move back. Note the approximate degree to which you have taken your top leg back from the horizontal.

RESULTS:
- **Under 45°** (below average)
- **45–60°** (average)
- **60–80°** (good)
- **Over 80°** (very good)

SQUAT TEST

Start in a standing position, with your knees about shoulder-width apart and hands stretched up above your head. Keeping your arms straight above your head, move slowly into a squat position as if lowering yourself onto a chair.

RESULTS:
- **Heels lifting off the ground indicate tight calf muscles.**
- **Knees positioned in front of your toes indicate weak glutes and overly developed quads.**
- **Either knee rolling inwards indicates weak hip abductors.**
- **Over-arching of lower back indicates tight hip flexors or weak core muscles.**

FOOT TEST

Place your bare foot on top of a tennis ball. With your weight on the ball, roll it from your heel down the middle of the foot towards your toes.

RESULTS:
- **No pressure or pain experienced during this test indicates good mobility of the tendons on the underside of the foot.**
- **Pressure or pain experienced during this test indicates poor mobility in the tendons on the underside of the foot.**

TOE PRONATION TEST

Stand as illustrated with your front knee positioned over your front ankle, your back leg straight and your weight evenly distributed between front and back foot. Without lifting your back foot, try to lift the toes of your back foot off the ground.

RESULTS: Inability to lift big toe off ground suggests pronation.

Ability to lift the big toe and small toes easily indicates neutral gait.

Big toe lifts easily and much higher than outer toes suggests supination.

CONCLUSIONS TO TESTS

• If on the **SQUAT TEST** you found that you had tight calf muscles and you did poorly on the **CALF/ACHILLES TEST**, then you should work on the flexibility of the calves by stretching before you increase the amount or intensity of your running. *To work on calf flexibility, see the stretching and mobility sections on pages 52–61.*

• If you struggled to perform the **SQUAT TEST** without the body leaning forward or the knees going out over the toes and you struggled in the **SINGLE LEG TEST** then you need to work on the strength of your glutes (the muscles in the bottom). The glutes play a vital role in controlling your movement and propulsion when running and without them functioning correctly it is almost impossible to run fast without putting strain on other parts of the body. *To work on the strength of your glutes, see the glute strength exercises in the exercise section on pages 164–187.*

• If you performed badly in the **HAMSTRING TEST** and/or the **LOWER BACK TEST**, then you need to work on the flexibility of the hamstring muscles and the hip and lower back area. Working on the flexibility of this area will give greater strength to the hamstrings and also prevent any lower back, pelvis and hamstring tightening and injury. *See the stretching exercises on pages 52–57 to work on these areas.*

• If your knees rolled inwards during the **SQUAT TEST** or if you performed poorly on the **HIP ABDUCTOR TEST**, you will need to build hip abductor strength into your routine to assist in the tracking of the knee during running and prevent the development of injuries such as runner's knee. *To work on the strength of your hip abductor, follow the foam rolling routines on pages 74-77, the mobility routines on pages 58-61 and the resistance programmes on pages 166–167.*

• If you performed badly at the **CORE TEST**, you will need to build core work into your routine. Core strength is vitally important in running – it is essential that the muscles of the abdominal section and the lower back are strong and hold the hips and the spine in a good position to allow the body to propel itself forward most effectively. *All of the strength programmes featured within the book have elements of core work within them, but check out the ab routines on page 167 for additional core exercises.*

• If you came out as average or below in the **CHEST TEST** or the **UPPER BACK TEST**, you will need to work on the range of motion of the upper body. The strength and mobility programmes will work on these areas. *Pay particular attention to the upper back exercises contained within the resistance programmes on pages 166–167.*

• If on the **FOOT TEST** you felt any tension under the foot, it could suggest a weakness of the muscles of the underside of the foot or tension held in the tendons under the foot. Any mild tension here would suggest that you need to start running in a well-structured running shoe with plenty of support. *If the tension is intense, then you may also need to work on strengthening the feet and reducing the tension by massage or using a roller, following the tips on pages 74–77.*

BREATHING TECHNIQUES

The ability to take on board the oxygen that your body demands in response to the challenges that you give it defines how well you run, how much you enjoy it, and how you will improve as a runner.

You might not have given thought to your breathing beyond the mental note of "Thank God I still am!" while running. However, like training your legs or mobilising your body, appropriate breathing techniques will help maximise your overall running performance and your enjoyment of it.

Breathing should come from the diaphragm and the lungs, so that you feel your upper stomach move as you breath in and out. Tensing the abdominal muscles might feel as though you are supporting a good upright stance but you are also limiting your ability to expand the lungs as well as you perhaps could.

Practise your breathing while sitting still and feel for the movement of the upper stomach area, beneath the base of the sternum (breast bone). Try to naturally let it move as you breathe, without forcing it. As you run, the relaxation of this point of the body will enable the potential of the lungs to be reached and will reduce the likelihood of muscular tension and discomfort building up in the shoulders, chest and neck areas, which are common problems for many runners.

If you can control your breathing while standing or sitting, there is no reason why you can't do so while running too. As you run, try to resist the temptation to rigidly hold the stomach tight. If your stomach muscles are strong enough already, they will be holding your posture in place without you thinking hard about it anyway.

Think of breathing as your fuel. Controlled breathing allows your body to recover quickly while you are pushing yourself further or faster. Tell yourself that the oxygen that you bring into your body in a controlled (rather than a rushed) way will re-energise your muscles again quickly and will allow you to keep pushing harder again soon.

In keeping with the relaxed but controlled running gait and style that we have covered previously, your breathing must not impinge on your posture. If you are gasping at air and tensing your chest and shoulders to do so, or lifting your head in a desperate reach for oxygen, your posture will be damaged and your running efficiency destroyed.

Technique is about control rather than force, and breathing is no exception. Controlled breathing may not feel relaxed at first – as you start a running routine you may well feel as though the lack of your lungs' ability to cope with the workload leaves you tense and struggling. In the very short term this could be difficult to avoid entirely, but you may simply need to slow down a little and focus on your form before you try to push too fast or too far.

BREATHING/STRIDE CADENCE RATIO

How many strides do you take for one breath in and for one breath out again? Don't know? This is your Breathing/Stride Cadence Ratio and now that you have relaxed your breathing pattern I want you start thinking about it. Next time you run, listen to the number of steps that you take as you breathe in and out and remember the pattern that you take naturally.

Once you have tested yourself you will know how many strides you are taking to breathe in and to breathe out as you run. While everyone varies slightly, I find that the following patterns work well for most people:

Slow Running	*3–4 strides to breathe in*
	3–4 strides to breathe out
Medium pace	*3 strides to breathe in*
	1–2 strides to breathe out
Fast pace	*2 strides to breathe in*
	1–2 strides to breathe out

As you increase your running pace, your body clearly needs more oxygen and will react by breathing faster and faster to keep up with the demand. This response is automatic; however, you will still be able to dictate the pace of your breathing within a narrow range.

You must find the pattern that works for you personally. I prefer to use an even breathing to stride pattern as I find it easier to regulate with the rhythm of the stride pattern. If you find, in using a pattern of 4 strides for your breathing, that you are tensing your shoulders or neck then you need to reduce the pattern or slow down your running speed. You need to regulate your breathing while always trying to keep as close as possible to a state of "homeostasis" (everything remaining the same) in the whole body.

Maximum intensity interval training sessions (see page 163) are a perfect time to practise with changes in breathing speed and give you a chance to adjust to the alterations in demand and supply in specific, controlled times.

Using your stride speed as a metronome for your breathing can become strangely hypnotic and is a good way of keeping your mind occupied as you run. The process of counting while listening to your breathing is a great distraction, while the compelling and almost obsessive nature of it will make you want to search out the breathing patterns that are best suited to you.

PACE CONTROL

Getting your pace right for any given distance of run is one of the hardest things to do, with failure to do so the reason for so many race-day disasters.

Pacing is all about practice and repetition so that you get to know how your body feels and performs at different intensities and in different situations. All too often we hear stories of how a runner went off too quickly feeling good and then eventually felt the effect of their efforts and finished the event slowly or, even worse, couldn't finish the race at all. Race day is *not* the day to test out how hard you can push yourself. That should be done during training and in a controlled manner.

Generally speaking, pacing is all about heart rate. While you are building up to being able to comfortably cover your chosen distance, pacing is about making sure that you are working at a good "aerobic" intensity where your body can comfortably supply you with the constant supply of energy that you need to carry out the work.

If you are running at anything over 10K, pacing is all about constantly looking at working within your comfort zone on the long runs and making sure that your body becomes more and more used to the distance, while always watching that you don't let your heart rate cross over into the anaerobic zone, where you will run out of energy quickly. Initially you should use your heart rate as a guide, before you start to look at your "mile splits" (the time it takes you to complete a mile). Many good club runners will work all their run strategies around mile splits. You may, for example, find that you can cope very well at 8 minutes per mile and from experience a 7.5 minute mile pace is just too fast. I like to work with a combination of mile splits and heart rates because I feel it gives me the most accurate gauge of whether I'm having a good or a bad day.

For shorter distance events you can afford to let your heart rate ride higher and be at the top end of your aerobic zone (and almost into your anaerobic zone). This is called anaerobic threshold running. The fitter you are, the longer you will be able to hold this level for; and the more you train at this level, the better the body becomes at reacting to this intensity.

What you always have to remember is that you can't get it right all of the time. Even those of us with years of experience have those race days where you get a bit excited, a bit competitive and end up pushing too hard and blowing up. That's part of racing and running!

OUT AND BACK

A great training routine for mastering pacing is called "Out and Back". The idea of this is to find a flat route that is half the length of your event and to run at race pace for that distance. Complete the distance and record the time. Then run back along the same route aiming to get back in the same time or less. If you have paced it right, you will get back in the same time or better. If you paced it wrong, it will take you longer to get back. Continually practising this type of little routine will help you get your pacing spot-on for race day.

THE PSYCHOLOGY OF RUNNING

Half the battle when trying to convince yourself to go for a run, work harder, or run further, lies in telling yourself that you *can* do it.

Our natural reaction to pain is to avoid it! Hit your hand while hammering nails and you pretty quickly adjust your approach to ensure that you are more careful next time. However, with running (and exercise generally) our relationship with pain is more complex. We know that the discomfort or "pain" is probably good for us so we endure the downside, to some degree, in order to reach the upside. Because we know that we might lose weight, or run further or faster, or perhaps win a race we are prepared to put up with a degree of pain that in any other context might have us calling for a doctor!

"I AM FIT AND HEALTHY"

Yet, despite the fact that we know the pain of exercise to be good for us, there are countless occasions where our bodies will try to convince us to stop. Pain in the legs, shortness of breath and feelings of reaching exhaustion are all strong reasons to make us think twice about running sometimes, and can also prevent us from pushing as hard as we potentially could to improve our performance.

It is at times like these that having a few mental techniques up our sleeves, like those detailed below, can prove extremely handy in helping us to keep going.

SELF-TALK

Positive self-talk is a powerful way of ensuring that you are fully ready and able to conquer whatever is thrown at you.

Talk to yourself in your head as you are running. Tell yourself you will feel great when you have finished. Tell yourself that the act of running itself makes you feel

"MY RUNNING IS STRONG"

lucky to be alive, fit and healthy enough to enjoy it. Also, remind yourself that what you are doing is fantastic for you now and for your future. You are doing a proactive, healthy thing that will prolong your life – feel proud about that! You can use any number of terms within a positive context as you like (a few good examples are given on this page and the next) but each self-talk phrase that you say to yourself *has* to be a positive message with no negatives. No "ifs", no "buts".

As we are more used to allowing negatives to focus the mind rather than allowing positives to influence us, this can be a tough practice for many people. However, the reality is that if you tell yourself that you are going to struggle, you *will* – a negative, defeatist attitude will make it far more difficult to get through the physical effort and demands that running places upon you.

While we can't help but let negatives enter our thoughts entirely (it is human nature after all) try to fight them off and keep a positive attitude throughout. Even when everything else is hurting, tell yourself that "it is better to try your very best and to fail, than to not ever try to give your best at all". Even in failure there are positives that you can draw from!

"I FEEL GOOD TODAY"

VISUALISATION

Imagine yourself on your run feeling well and strong, with great running posture. Think about how it feels to run well and then turn that thought into pictures in your mind. Now visualise the route of your run and consider how you will manage each section of it. If you know that there are hills in the run, picture them in advance so that you can prepare for how you will approach that challenge. Thoroughly map your run out so that you know how far you are going to go, what the terrain is like and have an understanding of what you are about to achieve.

How do you see yourself as a runner? Are you someone who looks like they are struggling through it? Think of yourself as a graceful runner who conserves and uses energy wisely. How does that look? Picture your stride pattern in detail – the strike of your foot on the ground, the number of strides you take and pattern of your breathing. Think about how it feels to breathe deeply and in control and visualise that too. Finally, picture yourself finishing your run too. Think how great you will feel when you get to the end of your training run or race and think about how that looks and feels.

You need to build a picture of yourself as a runner – a good one too! Remember, you are no different to anybody else and you can do just as much as everyone around you, so don't put limitations on yourself as you visualise your run.

GOAL SETTING

Like anything in life, you're far more likely to derive satisfaction and enjoyment from your running if you have a definite reason to keep going. You may find your motivation comes from reaching a particular set time or distance of run, or you may be focused on winning a race or getting as high a placement as possible. For many people these performance-related goals provide the powerful incentives they need. If you struggle to find that these goals give you the sense of purpose, however, you can always use other fallbacks to give you a nudge in the right direction.

Charity is the most obvious and well-used incentive for running in the world. Running raises enormous amounts of money for charity every year and provides a reason to train and run for all those who choose to enter an event on behalf of a charity. Having to complete a run for charity forces you to do the training for fear of letting down your sponsors, the cause, and yourself. It is a powerful pressure to complete your training.

"I CAN COMPLETE THE DISTANCE"

For many people, exercise is a means to ensure that they are healthy and well. Rather than achieving a set time or distance, your goal may be the knowledge that your heart and lungs, internal organs and bones all benefit from the exercise that running provides. You will only know how much you miss your health once it is gone, so focus on the fact that regular running will help keep you fit and healthy, alive for longer and with less illness along the way.

HITTING THE TRAINING WALL

There are times in everybody's training when the spark can just seem to have gone from their routine. Lethargy – both physical and mental – can cause mayhem with your ability to progress and improve, while every day that passes with you feeling unenthused will make your training sessions harder.

Overtraining is surprisingly common and not just in athletes but in regular enthusiastic exercisers too. It can manifest itself in a number of ways with symptoms ranging from physical tiredness and mental fatigue to aches, pains, changes in appetite and, of course, injury. Any one of these (or a combination) can make you feel both lousy and doubting your ability as to whether you can get back to where you were at your best.

Ask yourself questions of your routine to see if you can identify any problems...

ARE YOU TRAINING TOO MUCH WITHOUT RESTING? 5 or 6 days of training per week could be too much for your body to cope with if you are not managing your self-care effectively. If you are training to run a particular distance, follow the plans in this book and don't deviate and add more training just because you might feel good. The plans have been carefully designed to help you maximise your performance while ensuring that you make it to the end feeling your best.

ARE YOU EATING ENOUGH FOOD? If you are training hard, you will need to be consuming a pretty large number of calories, which could go against your natural tendency. If you are running regularly, your body will need roughly 35 calories per kg of bodyweight per day. Check the Diet and Hydration section of this book on pages 62–65 to establish whether or not you are eating the correct foods and drinking the necessary fluids to cope with your workload.

DO YOU GET ENOUGH SLEEP? You should be getting at least 6 hours undisturbed sleep per night. Be aware that alcohol, sugar and coffee will all disturb your sleep, so you may need to take steps to cut them out of your diet if this is the case.

ARE YOU DRINKING ENOUGH WATER? You need to drink about 1.5–2 litres per day, otherwise your body will be struggling far more than it needs to. While the body can survive on a lot less, we aren't talking about survival – we're talking about you feeling great and performing at your best.

ARE YOU CARRYING A NIGGLING INJURY? Even the smallest injury can make you feel as though you are struggling, making you move in a different way and leaving you more tired as a result. Use the advice on injury management contained within this book on pages 66–73 to help you manage the injury effectively.

If you have been through this list and you are *still* finding things tough, you will need think about your routine in a different way. The tips on the page opposite are the most effective ways I know to push up over that training hump and will get you enthused about running again. Take a look and try them out to get yourself back up to speed.

TOP TIPS FOR GETTING OVER THE TRAINING WALL

1. TAKE A BREAK

Literally, stop and have a few days off training. This will give your muscles a chance to recover and feel fresh again, while psychologically the break will give you the chance to not feel the pressures of performing to a strict routine.

2. DO SOMETHING DIFFERENT

Mix up your exercise routine for a couple of sessions per week. You might find that completely changing from say running to cycling for a week helps, or you may find that just changing route, terrain or distance is of benefit. For the more endurance-based exerciser, the idea of doing another 2–3 hour run can become a burden, so just shorten, lengthen or change the routine to break things up for a couple of days if you need to.

3. REMIND YOURSELF WHY YOU'RE DOING IT

We lose track sometimes and forget the reason we are training in the first place.

Is there a target date in mind, and when is it? Is there a weight-loss goal or a race time in mind? What is your motivation? Do you remember how far you have come in your workouts and physical changes so far? Look back at photos or think about your performances to see that you have come a long way and you have done really well so far. Now let's keep on going and do more!

4. REMEMBER HOW GREAT RUNNING CAN FEEL

Think of the moments in your runs when it all clicked and you felt great. When it felt as though every part of your body was working in tune and you could have kept going forever. You might not be feeling like that now, but it *will* happen again. Only so long as you keep running, that is.

5. BE CLEAR ABOUT YOUR TRAINING PLAN

Get your training mapped out on paper for the month ahead, as a diary plan. Distance plans are set out in this book but you need to set your own, personal targets on a weekly basis for achievement. These should be based around time, or speed – whatever motivates YOU. After each day is done, make notes about how you performed and what happened in your workout to your heart rate, your effort level, the speed you ran or anything else that you can compare back against in future. Use this to remind yourself how much you have progressed.

RUNNING GEAR

While you can go for a run anywhere and you don't need much more than a pair of running shoes to get started, the right gear can make all the difference between running and running well. Your running will be aided enormously if you can monitor your performance, if you can feed yourself when needed, if you have the appropriate clothing to feel comfortable physically and, also, if you look the part. While this last point might sound superficial, it isn't – looking and feeling like a runner is an important first step towards being one.

TRAINERS

This is the single most important piece of kit any runner will own. However, choosing the right pair of trainers for the type of running you do can be an absolute minefield –the range of shoes on the market is enormous and, depending on how much reading you do, the advice you can get can be utterly confusing.

So where do you start?

STEP 1. IDENTIFY THE TYPE OF RUNNING OR EVENT THAT YOU WANT TO DO.

For example, if you are planning on doing most of your running off-road or doing a forest trail-based event, say, then you will be able to concentrate straight away on looking at trail-based shoes. Most of the big brands now do trail shoes and there are also some great smaller companies who manufacture brilliant shoes just for this purpose. If, on the other hand, you are a relative newcomer to running and you plan to do a marathon for charity then, because of the miles you will have to cover in both training and in the event, you will need to have a shoe that is built with good structure and miles in mind. You may be a runner who runs regularly and now wants to concentrate on getting faster at 5K runs. For this type of work you probably want to save some of the weight of trainers and go for a race shoe that is light and helps you go fast. Whatever the case, choose the shoe to suit the event or type of running you will be doing.

STEP 2. WORK OUT WHAT YOU NEED PERSONALLY FROM A SHOE.

This is where it can get confusing and where you can easily be sold the wrong shoes. First things first, if you found from the Running Style Assessment on pages 26–33 that you had tight calf muscles, weak glutes or hamstrings, foot tendon sensitivity or back tightness, I would strongly recommend that you *do not* attempt full-on forefoot running, at least not until you score better on those tests and you have increased your flexibility and strength. In this case, any form of barefoot running shoe is out as you will need a trainer with good structure that does not allow too much movement throughout the running gait. Should you have a flat foot or have failed the Toe Pronation Test on page 32, then you will also need an element of anti-pronation control in your shoe.

If, on the other hand, you are an experienced runner and you scored well on all the running style tests then you can be a little more experimental in you choice of footwear; choosing a lighter-weight shoe with less stability control and therefore greater speed performance.

BAREFOOT RUNNING SHOES

So much has been written about barefoot running and a massive market has been established in shoes for this purpose. However, my feeling is that they do not offer enough support and cushioning for serious long-distance running. They should only be used by runners with perfect form, good strength and good mobility and only then if the runner tends to run on tracks that have some give in them, like forest routes. If you run in the city or if you have any strength and mobility issues that you need to work on, then barefoot running shoes should not be used.

Where these shoes can be very useful, however, is as a training aid. We could all benefit from making our feet stronger, as strong feet result in better-quality running. Using the barefoot shoe for walking about the house and doing short running drills in a park or on a track can really help to improve balance and propulsion. The only people who shouldn't even use them for this are those who discovered in the tests that they had tension in the tendon on the underside of the foot, or those who suffer from tight calf muscles.

MINIMALIST RUNNING SHOES

This relatively new category of running shoe for the experienced neutral-gait runner seems to be a good compromise between a typical running shoe and a barefoot variant. The idea behind this type of shoe is that it functions like a barefoot shoe, while still offering some structure and shock absorption. Importantly, the angle of drop from heel to toe on these shoes is closer to that of being barefoot and research shows that this enables a more natural running style to be adopted. Bear in mind, however, that it is still early days for this type of shoe, with most of the better-known brands only just launching their own versions now.

SHOE DO'S AND DON'TS

DO choose a shoe that performs well on the Rotation Test (see page 44) unless you performed well in all of the tests that make up the Running Style Assessment.
DO go to a specialist running shop to help choose your shoe – the chances are the sales people there will be runners themselves and will be able to advise you.
DO choose a shoe that feels comfortable and doesn't pinch the toes.
DO make sure that the shoe is well-ventilated and allows the foot to breathe.
DO make sure that the heel cup of the shoe supports and holds your heel.

DON'T buy the shoe that feels the bounciest. More bounce equals more potential injury.
DON'T run in shoes that were clearly designed for fashion rather than running!
DON'T be up-sold the most expensive shoes in the shop.
DON'T buy shoes that feel heavy on your feet. (Running properly requires quick moving feet and this will be very difficult if your legs feel heavy.)

SHOE ROTATION TEST

Unless you are a strong, experienced runner with a perfectly neutral foot type and no biomechanical weaknesses you'll need a shoe that that protects you from over-rotating on landing. The best way to test this is to hold your shoe as shown in the pictures and see how easily it rotates. If your foot pronates or supinates, you should choose a shoe with no more movement in the rotation test than demonstrated in the first picture. If you have a neutral foot you could go for a shoe that rotates as much as the middle picture. Never choose a show that rotates as much as the picture on the right.

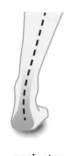

pronator　　**neutral runner**　　**supinator**

HEEL INVERSION TEST

For this test you will need a partner to assess you. Stand in a normal, relaxed stance after having walked on the spot a couple of times and get your partner to look at your heels from behind. Now get them to see which of these pictures most closely relates your foot. If the line of the heel bone appears to be leaning into the middle of the body like the image on the left it is most likely that your foot pronates. If the line of the heel looks straight up like the image in the middle it suggest you have a neutral foot type. If the line of the body appears to move away from the body as in the image on the right it would suggest that you supinate.

pronator　　**neutral runner**　　**supinator**

ARCH HEIGHT TEST

When you get out of the shower, put a foot on the bathmat and look at the imprint it makes. If there is little or no arch you probably have a flat foot and therefore a tendency to pronate. If you have a neutral arch you'll see a wider arch connecting the heel and forefoot and more than likely you neither pronate nor supinate. If you have high arches you'll see a narrow imprint connecting heel and forefoot, suggesting you might supinate.

OTHER THINGS YOU MIGHT NEED

HEART-RATE MONITOR
To train smarter as well as harder, you really need a heart-rate monitor. These
vary from – at their most basic – units that provide your working heart rate and a
stopwatch, to the fanciest of monitors that will also give you your running speed,
global position, altitude, temperature and can chart and analyse your results in
much greater depth. Which one you go for is up to you and your wallet! If you
intend to run for fun and to take part in occasional 5K runs, you may find that a
basic unit will fulfil your need to monitor your intensity and track your run time.
However, if you are more intent on running longer distances, and certainly if you
intend to keep achieving new personal best performances, you should buy the most
advanced watch you can afford. Using the data that a top-end monitor provides,
particularly current speed and distance figures, is incredibly motivating – as is the
ability to download the information to your computer to track and log your runs.
Perhaps the only discussion would be whether to go for a GPS-based unit or a
monitor with a foot pod to track your speed. From personal experience, I would opt
for the foot pod as I have found them to be more accurate in general. I am sure they
will continue to change, but GPS-based watches still lose signal occasionally, which
can be annoying!

WATER CARRIERS
The further you are going to run, the more you are going to need hydration. If you
are running 5K, you can probably survive without water, but once you are running
10K and beyond your performance will dip if you don't re-stock on fluids.

For longer distances, hand-held water bottles are available that are shaped to allow
you to grip "through" the bottle. These provide enough fluid to last you for around
45–75 minutes and are perfectly good to run with, provided you feel comfortable
running while holding onto something in one or both hands.

If you are running for longer than 75 minutes, you should consider buying a belt
with a built-in bottle holder. The bottles they hold generally have a capacity of
around 500ml, which should be adequate for a run of up to around 90–120 minutes,
or a distance of 12–20K.

Once you go beyond running a half-marathon distance, you will need to carry more
water than is comfortable or practical to hold in your hands or a belt. In this case
you should consider training using a backpack water carrier. These feature a plastic
fillable "bladder" in the small rucksack with a tube that feeds towards your mouth
that you can reach for at any time. While the process of running and sucking on a
tube can feel strange at first, it is by far and away the most convenient and effective
way to hydrate yourself as you train for your longer-distance runs. These packs
also have room to hold food and energy gels if needed, as well as your iPod and
house keys (and maybe some emergency taxi money too!).

CLOTHING

To run effectively, you do need the correct clothes. If you get cold you will not be able to perform, and if you have clothes flapping around you will certainly be restricted. Clothes need to be fitted but comfortable. Choose materials that breathe and stretch. This almost certainly means man-made fabrics. For some this might seem counter-intuitive, but these artificial fabrics are designed to work for your needs – wicking moisture away from your body and allowing heat to escape when needed, while maintaining it when desired. Depending on the weather, running leggings, shorts, vests, shower-proof jackets, hats, gloves and specific socks may all be part of your everyday running wardrobe.

In the winter you should have two pairs of running leggings available – one heavyweight and one lightweight as needed. Compression-based leggings have the benefit of increasing the supply of blood to your heart and therefore may increase recovery speed and decrease fatigue while running. You will also need a long-sleeved fitted T-shirt and I would recommend that you try specifically designed ranges using high-performance fabrics. To keep your neck warm, you should wear a fine fleece layer over the top with a high zip neck and, for when it rains, you will need to have a jacket of some type – ideally one made from a breathable water-resistant fabric such as Goretex or Teflon. Try to use this only when it actually rains as you may find yourself overheating at other times. Complete your winter outfit with some thin running gloves and, if you find that your neck gets particularly cold, a snood (a type of tubular neck scarf).

In the summer, girls should choose between crop leggings or running shorts while guys should choose running shorts – sticking with the running brands which produce some very good shorts that are designed with supportive "inner" shorts. Your choice of sock is also important. Choose from the specific running compression socks that are on the market and help circulation, or regular socks with in-built cushioning.

MUSIC

If you prefer to run to music, simply take your iPod or MP3 player with you. Buy a suitable strap for your arm (so that you don't have to carry it around in your hand) and get some headphones that have in-built ear clips so they don't fall off as you run. Pick your playlist (keep it upbeat as this will improve performance) and away you go.

UP AND RUNNING

WARMING UP AND COOLING DOWN

A lot of runners put on their kit, tie up their shoes and start running. In a way there is nothing greatly wrong with doing this, provided you start running slowly and gradually build up to full pace over several minutes, and provided you don't feel at all stiff or fatigued, suffer from any slight postural imbalance or mind your performance not being as good as it could be.

If, however, you want to reduce the likelihood of injury and run at your best (and I suspect you do, given that you are reading this) then you really do need to spend some time preparing for what is, after all, a pretty tough examination of your body. After all, no professional athlete – no matter what their sport – would launch themselves straight into competition without giving themselves the fullest preparation possible, and you should be no different.

Warming up is a process of increasing the body temperature, circulation, blood vessel dilation, joint mobility, muscle elasticity and mental focus – all of which combine to play an important role in improving how we feel when we actually start running. By increasing your body temperature through movement with drills, runs or mobility exercises, we are aiming to raise the ability of the body to carry blood and oxygen to those areas that need it. This gradual increase in working level will start working your cardio-respiratory system; dilating your capillaries and enabling them to carry blood more freely which, in turn, will provide your muscles with the glycogen and oxygen that they need to keep up with demand.

MOBILITY ROUTINES

Mobility routines allow the major joints to move through a long range of motion, enforce an active stretch onto the surrounding muscle tissues and are great ways to warm up the body. They are particularly useful for the knees, where they encourage the synovial fluid, the "oil" that protects the knee joints, to be produced. Although we run on our legs, our arms, spine and pelvis are all involved in the action of running, so these areas are also included in the routines listed on the following pages.

STRETCHING

Though there is ongoing debate within fitness circles about the need for pre-activity stretching of the muscles, I believe that it should be a key part of your warm-up and cool-down routines. While in theory your muscles might stretch and adjust as you take your first strides, for most of us there is every chance that we are starting with a bit of residual stiffness – whether through over-activity, under-activity or just as a result of getting older! With this in mind the muscles need to be stretched before you run after you have completed the mobility routines. Whether you are running for 10 minutes or 5 hours, you should spend several minutes stretching both before and after your run. What matters is that once you take those first few pounding strides you are not going to be anything other than able to cope and ready to perform.

STRETCHES

Ideally, you should do this gentle stretching programme before and after each run. It should take no more than 10 minutes – time well spent to insure yourself against future problems. Post-exercise stretching is important as exercise causes your muscles to contract and shorten, actually reducing flexibility. Stretching after exercise, when muscles are warmed up and as a result more responsive, reduces this shortening and helps to disperse lactic acid that builds up during a workout, while also significantly reducing the risk of injury.

STANDING HAMSTRING STRETCH

In a standing position, raise your right leg and place the heel on a rail or bench. Lean forward, keeping your back and legs straight and your shoulders and pelvis facing forwards throughout. Hold the stretch for as long as necessary. Repeat with the opposite leg.

Pre-workout:
8–10 secs each leg

Post-workout:
15–20 secs each leg

STANDING GLUTE STRETCH

Stand a foot away from a bench or wall. Holding the bench with your left hand, cross your right ankle over your left thigh and rest it against the bench. Making sure your back is straight, rest your right hand on your right thigh and hold the stretch for as long as necessary. Repeat with the opposite leg.

Pre-workout:
8–10 secs each leg
Post-workout:
15–20 secs each leg

FRONT FACING ITB AND GLUTE STRETCH

Stand about an arm's length from a post or wall. Place your right hand on the post and position your right foot directly in front of your left. Press your hips to the right towards the post, keeping your legs straight. Hold the stretch for as long as necessary. Switch sides and repeat with the opposite leg.

Pre-workout:
8–10 secs each leg
Post-workout:
15–20 secs each leg

CALF STRETCH

Stand with your right foot forward and left foot a step-width behind. With your toes pointing ahead, slightly bend your right knee (moving your weight forward), keeping your left knee straight and your heels on the floor. Hold the stretch for as long as necessary before repeating on the other leg.

Pre-workout:
8–10 secs each leg
Post-workout:
15–20 secs each leg

QUAD STRETCH

Stand up straight, keeping your left, supporting leg slightly bent. Bend your right leg and, holding the front of your foot, pull your foot up towards your bottom. Keep your knees together, your hips pointing forwards and your back as straight as possible. Hold the stretch for as long as necessary before repeating on the other leg.

Pre-workout:
8–10 secs each leg
Post-workout:
15–20 secs each leg

HAMSTRING STRETCH OFF KNEE

In a kneeling position, extend your left leg straight ahead of yourself, resting your heel on the ground. Lean forward, keeping your back straight, your knee extended and your shoulders and pelvis facing forwards throughout. Hold the stretch for as long as necessary before repeating with the opposite leg.

Pre-workout:
6–8 secs each leg
Post-workout:
15–20 secs each leg

CAT STRETCH

Go down on your hands and knees, keeping your back straight. Push your spine upwards to create a curve in the middle of your back. Hold the position for as long as necessary, then return to the start position.

Pre-workout:
Raise and hold for 1 sec. Lower for 1 sec. Repeat 10–12 times
Post-workout:
As above

HIP FLEXOR

Kneel on both knees. Step forwards with your left foot keeping your right knee on the floor. Place your hands on either side of your front foot. Slide your back leg out behind you until you feel the stretch in the front of your hip. Push your hip forwards, straighten your body and place your hands on your front knee. Hold the stretch for as long as necessary and repeat for the other side.

Pre-workout:
8–10 secs each leg
Post-workout:
15–20 secs each leg

LOWER BACK STRETCH

Lie on your back. Holding the tops of your shins, bring both knees in towards your body. Gently pull your knees in closer until you feel the stretch in your lower back. Hold for as long as necessary.

Pre-workout:
6–8 secs
Post-workout:
15–20 secs

PRONE CHEST STRETCH

Lie down on your left side with your knees bent directly beneath your body. Reach your right arm out straight to the side, rotating the upper body without moving the hips and legs. Feel the stretch in the chest and upper arm. Hold the stretch for as long as necessary before repeating on the other side.

Pre-workout:
8–10 secs each side
Post-workout:
15–20 secs each side

LOWER BACK ROTATION

Lie on your back with your arms outstretched at shoulder level. Bend your right leg and place the right foot over the left knee. Slowly twist to the left with your left hand gently pressing down on the right knee and the right arm extended to your side. Relax into the stretch and feel it in your lower back and hips. Hold for as long as necessary before repeating on the opposite side.

Pre-workout:
4–6 secs each side
Post-workout:
15–20 secs each side

MOBILITY DRILLS

The mobility drills outlined here should be attempted after you have finished your initial stretches. These movements will prepare the body for any form of exercise; however, you will notice a big improvement in your running ability after completing them, as they increase the flexibility and therefore the mobility of the body.

This series of exercises is designed to stimulate the main muscles you will be using while running as well the main postural muscles you use during your everyday life which suffer tension and need to be mobilised before your workout. Many of us live fairly sedentary lifestyles and muscles such as the hip flexors and the lower back lose mobility and commonly suffer from a high degree of tension. This series of exercises, performed regularly, will give you some of that range of motion back in the most commonly suffering areas. This is perhaps one of the most overlooked parts of most runners' preparation, yet any athlete would not dream of missing it out, so why should *you* be any different?

HIP FLEXOR REACH
Kneel on the right leg with your left leg out in front and your left foot flat on the floor. The front knee should be bent at 90° to the hip. Push the hips forward and at the same time reach with your arms up above your head. The torso should be straight and upright. Keep your abs tight to prevent unwanted movement in the lower back. Repeat on the other side.

SPIDERMAN

Start in a press-up position, making sure your abs stay tight and that your hands are directly beneath your shoulders. Bring your right foot up to the outside of your right hand. Try to maintain a straight back by bringing your chest up as you step forward. Hold this position for 2–3 seconds. Repeat on the other side.

TRUNK ROTATION

Sit upright with your arms outstretched on each side of the body. Bring your right leg up to hip height. Keeping the left leg straight, take the right leg across the left knee. Use the left hand to press down on the right outer knee. Repeat on the opposite side.

REVERSE LUNGE WITH REACH

Start in a standing position with your back straight and your feet shoulder-width apart. Step backwards, bending both knees to 90° and maintaining a straight torso. As you step back, bring your arms straight up alongside your body and finish with them straight above your head. You should feel a stretch in your hip flexors and shoulder/upper back area. Push straight back up to the starting position, taking a step forwards and returning your hands to your sides. Repeat on the opposite side.

GLUTE SWINGS

Stand sideways close to a wall with your weight on your left leg and your left hand on the wall for balance. Swing your right leg forward and backward, maintaining a straight back, before repeating on the other side.

HIP FLEXOR SWINGS

Leaning slightly forward with both hands on a wall and your weight on your left leg, swing your right leg to the left in front of your body. Swing your leg back across your body, pointing your toes upwards as your foot reaches its furthest point of motion. Repeat on the other side.

WALL ANGELS

Stand with your back against a wall and your feet a step forward. Roll your pelvis forwards and backwards until you are happy that you have found your mid-position (neutral pelvis). Keep your hands against the wall at shoulder height with your palms facing away from you. Raise your arms to shoulder height to create a 'Y' shape. Holding this position, pull your shoulder blades down and in while bringing your elbows down towards your sides. Try to keep your arms and hands as close to the wall as possible.

DIET AND HYDRATION

If you are training regularly for any exercise or sport, it is vital that you are able to perform feeling as though you are not depleted. Diet plays a key part in this. There is nothing worse than recognising that physically your fitness was fine to push to a higher limit, but your preparation (or lack of it), let you down when you needed it most.

PRE-RUN DIET

Eating prior to running is as important as putting fuel into a car before driving. To provide your body with the energy you require, you will need to consume food that is rich in carbohydrates – the body's main source of working energy. (Although your body also converts and utilises fats and proteins as needed, it is carbohydrates that are its real rocket fuel and will give you the energy you need.) The foods you choose to eat before you exercise should be things that:

• are rich in carbohydrate
• are low in fat
• are easy to digest
• include some fluid (for example, fruit)
• are things you like to eat regularly

Ideally you should choose to eat foods that have a combination of low- and high-GI (Glycaemic Index) ratings before exercising. Low- to moderate-GI foods will provide you with sustained slow-release sugars throughout your training or competition run and should be the mainstay of your diet, with no more than 10–15% coming from high-GI sources. A table of GI food examples is shown below.

THE GLYCAEMIC INDEX		
Low-GI Foods	**Medium-GI Foods**	**High-GI Foods**
Apples, apricots, berries, cherries, dates, figs, gooseberries, grapes, kiwis, limes, mangoes, melons, papaya, passion fruit, pears	Pineapple, strawberries	Honey, syrup
	Milk, soya milk, rice milk	White potatoes, parsnips
Asparagus, aubergine, broccoli, Brussels sprouts, cabbage, carrots, cauliflower, celery, chicory, cucumber, courgettes, ginger, leeks, peppers, sweet potato, squash, spinach	Wholemeal bread, wholemeal pasta, brown rice, couscous, oats, puffed rice, puffed millet	Bananas, dried fruit
	Sunflower seeds, pumpkin seeds	White bread, white pasta, basmati rice
Millet, quinoa, wild rice	Sweetcorn	Chocolate, biscuits, sweetened yoghurt, sweetened cereals, jam and spreads
Butter beans, chickpeas, haricot beans, kidney beans, lentils, peas, soya beans		
Almonds, brazil nuts, chestnuts, sesame seeds		

TOO FULL TO RUN?

If you are worried about feeling too "full" before running – a common complaint – try eating a "solid" meal comprised mainly of low- to moderate-GI foods plus some protein around 2–3 hours before you run, before switching to fluid-based nutrition in the form of smoothies or a good commercial carbohydrate powder drink. The rapidly digested nature of these drinks will leave you feeling less full or bloated, but you should be aware that it is more difficult to consume as many calories using this approach, so you may need to work harder on your strategy for eating during your run if you are planning on going for longer than 60 minutes.

WHAT TO DRINK BEFORE RUNNING?

When running for more than around 30 minutes, your hydration will define your ability to run well, therefore pre-run hydration should be a crucial factor in your planning. As your body struggles to take on as much fluid as it loses through sweating while exercising, a decent start point is vital. In a normal day you should be drinking 1.5–2 litres of water. Make sure you have taken on at least 300ml of water in the hour before running – this should be in addition to your normal water intake. Avoid stocking up on energy drinks before you run as you are better served by good food and plain water at this point.

MORNING EXERCISE

If you are exercising in the morning, as many people choose to, you will have just been through a "fasting" period overnight in which your body has not been fuelled and your glycogen levels have been allowed to drop. As with any prolonged period without eating prior to exercise, this will have an extreme adverse effect on your energy and performance level. You should therefore ensure that you eat the appropriate food a minimum of 60 minutes and ideally 90–120 minutes before exercise to give yourself the optimum chance of feeling ready to exert your body as required

ULTRA-DISTANCE NUTRITION

At the outer end of the endurance scale, as we look at ultra-distance events of four hours plus, the nutritional demands placed on the body are enormous. Because exercise takes place at a lower level for a longer period, the body is more readily able to take on and digest solid foods efficiently. Also, besides the enormous amount of carbohydrate that is required and burnt away during extreme-distance training and competing, there is also a slightly increased requirement for protein as the body reaches the outer limits of ability and fatigue and existing glycogen stores begin to run out. Energy requirements for ultra-distance events are enormous and can easily be as much as 4,000–5,000 calories per day. You will therefore need an array of good-quality muesli bars, high-quality carbohydrate and protein drink solutions and snacks such as jam sandwiches, bananas and biscuits to keep you going. If you are taking part in an ultra-distance event, I suggest that you see a dietician or good sports nutritionist who can tailor your nutrition to meet your specific requirements, as you are clearly pushing yourself to an extreme level.

REFUELLING ON THE MOVE

During your run your body will use up a mixture of glycogen (carbohydrates) and fats.

If you are running for less than 1 hour, you have no need to worry about eating during your run – your body can adequately provide the energy you need from its stores for around 45–75 minutes depending upon the individual and the intensity of the training.

FOOD

If you are running for longer than 90 minutes, you will need to restock your glycogen supply. There are many different choices that runners make about their eating plans, from sugary sweets to oat bars and flapjacks and from gel packs to bananas. Eating on the run is a bit of a skill and there will be a routine that you find works for YOU. For some, eating specific commercial gels or sugar drinks brings on uncomfortable and upset stomachs; for others, these are precisely what is required. While sugary sweets might sound appealing (and you may even get a craving for this instant sugar hit after a couple of hours), they can actually make you feel a bit zapped in the minutes that follow and leave you feeling "empty". I have found half a banana every 20 minutes following the first 75 minutes works, alongside a sports drink (330ml) every hour after the first hour to work best for me, but try a few different options to see what works best for you. As an idea of the quantity you might need, studies have pointed towards an amount of 30–60g of carbohydrates needing to be consumed after the first hour of performance to maintain levels.

FLUIDS

Your body stores an enormous amount of fluids; however, we start burning these the moment we start working harder. Just a small amount of dehydration can cause a marked drop in performance, water can't wait until you finish anything other than a run of up to 30 minutes in length. A sports drink provides some carbohydrate as sugars and can help delay fatigue in a run of up to 90 minutes.

POST-RUN NUTRITION

After you have completed a training session or a competition you will have used energy and fluids from a few sources. You now need to quickly replace some of the lost elements to ensure that you a) allow your muscles to recover quickly and b) feel "normal" as soon as possible after becoming depleted.

FLUIDS

Fluids are perhaps the most important priority to focus on, as even becoming slightly dehydrated will make you feel unwell, slow muscle recovery and could make your ability to perform even simple tasks more difficult. Hopefully you will have used a good hydration programme while running, but it is important to ensure that you are fully rehydrated now, so you should drink between 0.25 and 0.5 litres of fluid within the first 30 minutes after running. You might want to experiment with commercial recovery drinks that contain an array of minerals and sugar, or perhaps with diluted juices or fresh smoothies, though you will be fine drinking plain water.

FOOD

After exercise you have a 30-minute "window of opportunity" in which you should try to eat an appropriate type of snack or meal. While your body will need the food within 2 hours to ensure that you recover without any adverse effects, it is the first 30 minutes that present the greatest opportunity to avoid any dip in blood sugar and to re-stock the lost glycogen in the body at the quickest rate possible.

Ideally, after exercise your choice of snack or meal should be high in carbohydrate and moderate in protein and you should take on plenty of fluids either within your food or separate, or both. It may simply be a case of snacking to replenish your reserves straight away, to be followed by a larger meal containing carbohydrates, proteins and fats later, particularly if you are considering training more than once in the day or if you have to rush back to work or don't have time to eat a great deal of food. Whatever you do, *do not* skip eating after exercise – it is completely counter-productive.

In terms of quantity you should be trying to replenish your reserves at a rate of around 1–2g of carbohydrates per kg of bodyweight within the first two hours of finishing your run. For most people this means consuming 70–180g of carbs in the intial 2 hours.

Finishing a run does not mean "I deserve to eat whatever I like as a treat!". Instead, it is best viewed as a time to refuel your body. That said, you should, of course, choose foods that you enjoy eating – provided they fit the bill!

EXAMPLES OF GOOD POST-RUN SNACKS

• Banana sandwich

• Fresh fruit

• Fruit juice

• Fruit bar

• Low-fat flavoured yoghurt

• Fresh fruit salad with low-fat yoghurt or low-fat dairy dessert

• Smoothie or soy-smoothie made from reduced-fat milk, low-fat yoghurt and banana, mango or berries

TOP 5 OVER-USE
RUNNING INJURIES

- ITB Friction Syndrome

- Achilles Tendonitis/ Tendonopathy

- Plantar Fascitis

- Runner's Knee

- Shin Splints

RUNNING INJURIES

HOW TO SPOT THEM, WHEN TO TREAT THEM AND HOW TO PREVENT THEM

It is a common misconception that running is "bad for your joints". While running badly will inevitably cause problems, with good technique, a structured training plan and the right equipment there is no reason why you should let this bother you.

Depending on which source you read, running-related injury is quoted as affecting anywhere between 24 and 77% of all runners. Experience suggests that almost all runners will experience pain or discomfort to some degree as a result of their training. Yet, while there is an undeniable injury risk associated with running, there is much that can be done to prevent and treat these problems. This section will help you to understand why injury may occur so that you can implement strategies to reduce your injury risk, identify the early signs of potential problems in order to offset them and effectively treat injury to lessen the impact on your training.

As you can see then, injury associated with running is not uncommon and it is likely that in the course of your running career you will experience one. If you have identified potential problems before they arise, you will significantly reduce your injury risk. Prevention is always better than cure!

Potential problems should be addressed with particular attention to your:

• **FOOTWEAR**
• **TRAINING PLAN**
• **STRENGTH AND CONDITIONING TO SUPPLEMENT YOUR RUNNING**
• **REST**
• **NUTRITION AND HYDRATION**

In the event that a problem does arise, acting early to indentify the cause and site of the problem will limit the severity and the impact of the injury. Injury does not have to have a significant impact on your training plan. Sometimes people are reluctant to seek expert help for fear that they will be told to stop running. A good practitioner with a special interest in sports injury will do their utmost to keep you on track for your goals. A period of relative rest may be necessary, but there is almost always another area of your training that you can focus on while you are waiting for the problem to resolve.

OVER-USE INJURY

The majority of running injuries are caused by over-use. When we exercise, our body is subjected to stresses which we call "micro trauma" and, as we rest and recover, our body heals – becoming stronger as a result of our actions. Where the body's ability for repair is equal to the demands placed upon it, no injury occurs. It is this fine balancing act which allows us to improve our fitness and performance.

When your body is not able to keep up with the repair demands that are placed upon it and the balance between recovery and activity is tipped, then damage occurs. This type of injury is known as an over-use injury, and is the type we most commonly see in runners. The next few pages detail the five most common over-use running injuries, how to spot them and what to do about them.

P.R.I.C.E.

The list of over-use injuries featured within this section is by no means exhaustive. Most running injuries are preventable but accidents *do* and *will* happen. If you are unlucky to fall foul of an over-use injury or if any other accident or injury occurs then there are some general principles that you can apply immediately to help treat the problem. These principles are commonly referred to as P.R.I.C.E and are most helpful in the first 48–72 hours after onset of pain or injury.

Using these immediate first aid measures can help relieve pain, limit swelling and protect the injury, all of which will help the healing process. If you are at all unsure or if the problem does not begin to resolve itself within 12–24 hours, you should seek medical advice.

PROTECTION

Protect the injured site from further injury. Exactly how you go about doing this depends on the area that has been damaged – crutches, slings, braces, splints and taping are all effective protective supports.

REST

It is important to rest the injured area during the early phase of healing as this prevents the area being stressed. When you first start moving the area again, avoid excessively stressing the healing tissue.

ICE

Putting ice on an injury, no matter how small, will do wonders to ease it by reducing internal swelling and numbing any pain. The best way to do so is to wrap crushed ice, frozen veg or an ice compress in a damp towel before applying it to the skin. The damp towel keeps the ice from coming into direct contact with the skin, which can lead to ice burn. Ice for 20–30 minutes, repeating approximately every two hours until the swelling and/or "heat" from the injury is reduced.

COMPRESSION

Apply strapping or a tubular bandage (a pressure stocking) to the affected area as soon as possible following the injury to reduce swelling in the joint and to keep it stable. Remove this support before sleeping.

ELEVATION

Elevate the injured area above the level of the heart to prevent blood pooling there and so reduce swelling and discomfort. Support the injured limb with a cushion for comfort. (N.B. Do not compress and elevate the afflicted area at the same time, as this has the potential to reduce the blood flow too much.)

ITB FRICTION SYNDROME

ITB friction syndrome, sometimes also referred to as iliotibial band syndrome, is characterised by pain on the outside of the knee joint. This pain is often worse when going up or down stairs.

The iliotibial band (ITB or IT band) is a sheath of thick, fibrous connective tissue which helps to straighten the knee joint as well as to move the hip out sideways. It attaches at the top of the thigh to both the hip bone (iliac crest) and a muscle called the tensor fasciae latae, and then runs down the outside of the thigh and joins onto the outer surface of the shin bone (tibia). If the iliotibial band is tight or stiff it rubs as it runs over the outside of the knee joint, resulting in the symptoms listed below.

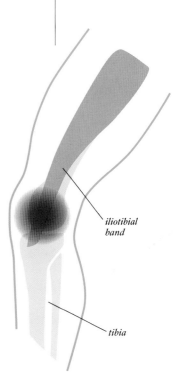

iliotibial band

tibia

SYMPTOMS
- **Dull aching or burning sensation on the outside of the knee during activity**
- **Sharp stabbing pain on the outside of the knee during activity**
- **Pain may be localised, but generally radiates around the outside of the knee and/or up the outside of the thigh**
- **Pain typically starts as minor discomfort and worsens progressively**
- **Snapping, creaking, or popping may occur when the knee is bent and then straightened**
- **There is usually no swelling**
- **Pain is worse when going downstairs or downhill**

CAUSES
While over-use is a secondary or aggravating factor of ITB friction syndrome, the underlying cause is often poor technique. Refer back to pages 26–33 and assess your running style to identify where you may have a problem and how to address the issue. You should also consider your choice of footwear and the volume of training as possible causes, and make changes to these as necessary.

TREATMENT
- Use the P.R.I.C.E principles as initial treatment for the pain and inflammation (see opposite).
- Massage will help to improve this problem. You can use a foam roller to achieve this effect at home (see page 76).

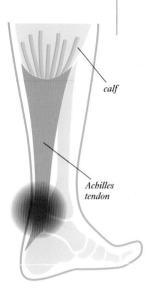

calf

Achilles tendon

ACHILLES TENDONITIS/TENDONOPATHY

Achilles tendonitis or Achilles tendonopathy are both terms used to describe pain arising from the Achilles tendon that is felt at the back of the heel and lower leg.

Tendons attach muscle to bone and the calcaneal tendon, more commonly known as the Achilles tendon, attaches the calf muscles to the heel bone (calcaneus).

It is the strongest and thickest tendon in the body; however, it is particularly vulnerable to over-activity and over-stressing, which leads to the development of tendonopathy.

Injury to the Achilles tendon occurs when the load applied to the tendon, either in a single episode or more often over a period of time, exceeds the tendon's ability to withstand that load.

SYMPTOMS

- **Pain localised to the Achilles tendon**
- **Onset of pain is gradual**
- **Pain is worse in the morning or after activity**

Some people may also notice a thickening of the tendon – this can be present without much pain. You may also notice a nodule (small lump) over the tendon, or a creaking noise when moving.

H.A.R.M.

As well as things that you should do to treat injury there are also things that you should avoid in the first day or two after an injury (see below). Avoid all of these as they may make the problem worse and prolong your recovery. Although applying heat to running injuries might appear to soothe aches and pains, it will be having exactly the opposite effect to ice and will make things worse.

HEAT

ALCOHOL

RETURN TO ACTIVITY

MASSAGE

TREATMENT

- Use the P.R.I.C.E. principles as initial treatment for inflammation (see page 68).
- Stretching the muscles that are attached to the Achilles is vital (see pages 52–57) to alleviate stress.

CAUSES

The most common cause of Achilles injury is over-use. Excessive mileage, sudden increases in training intensity, incorrect footwear, poor running style and inadequate warm-up/cool-down can all act as contributing factors. Any predisposition to tendon injury is largely related to biomechanics – the Achilles tendon is susceptible to a bowstring or whipping effect if the foot has a tendency to roll inwards. Those who have tight and/or weak calf muscles are particularly at risk.

PLANTAR FASCITIS

Plantar fascitis is a typical runners' injury and is one of the most common causes of heel pain. It is the inflammation of the plantar fascia, the connective tissue that runs from the heel down each side of the foot to the toes.

plantar fascia

SYMPTOMS

- **Pain anywhere on the underside of the foot, from the heel to the arch. The main source of pain is often found about 4 cm forward from the heel, and may be tender to the touch.**
- **Pain is often worst when taking your first steps in the morning, or after long peri‌‌‌ e no weight is placed on your f‌‌‌‌ pain, but being on your feet for long**
- ‌‌‌ **ur foot (e.g. walking up stairs or on tip-** t‌‌‌

CAU‌

Plan‌‌‌‌‌‌ plantar fascia at the point where it joins onto ‌‌‌‌‌ low-arched foot can predispose you to planta‌‌‌‌‌ n runners, it can also be caused by non-suppo‌‌‌‌‌ cles at the back of the leg.

You are‌‌‌ ‌‌ia if:
- You ar‌‌‌‌‌ you do lots of walking, running, standing‌‌‌
- You hav‌‌‌‌‌ rent surface.
- You hav‌‌‌‌‌ ning or poor arch support.
- You are d‌‌‌ n your heel).
- There is o‌‌‌‌‌ our sole. For example: athletes who increase ru‌‌‌ or distance; poor technique starting "off the blocks", etc.
- You have a tight Achilles tendon.

TREATMENT

- Use the P.R.I.C.E. principles as initial treatment (see page 68).
- Choose shoes with cushioned heels and a good arch support. Avoid old or worn shoes (especially sports shoes) that may not give a good cushion to your heel.
- Invest in heel pads and arch support inserts for your shoes. Place the inserts/pads in both shoes even if you only have pain in one foot.
- Regular, gentle stretching of your Achilles tendon and plantar fascia may help to ease your symptoms. Use a foot roller to massage the undersurface of the foot in order to stretch and mobilise the plantar fascia.
- When you are asleep, your plantar fascia tends to tighten up (which is why it is usually most painful first thing in the morning). A splint can be worn overnight to keep the plantar fascia stretched while you sleep.

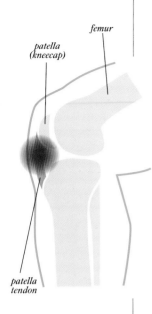

femur

patella (kneecap)

patella tendon

RUNNER'S KNEE

Runner's knee is also known as patello-femoral syndrome or anterior knee pain. It causes pain at the front of the knee, which is often described by sufferers as coming from behind the kneecap.

SYMPTOMS
- **Pain beneath or on the sides of the kneecap**
- **A grinding noise as the rough cartilage rubs when the knee is bent**
- **Swelling of the knee**
- **Pain going up or down stairs/hills**

CAUSES

Runner's knee is usually a result of the kneecap's inability to "track" properly. Tracking refers to the path that the kneecap takes as it slides over a groove on the thighbone (femur) as your knee bends and straightens. When bending and straightening, several structures surrounding the knee joint act together to cause the kneecap to run in a straight line within the groove. If any of the structures that act around the knee are particularly tight or weak, this causes an imbalance which can pull the kneecap to the left or right of the groove, causing pressure, friction, and irritation to the cartilage on the undersurface of the kneecap when the knee is in motion.

This type of problem can also occur following any other knee injury, if the quadricep muscles in the leg have become weakened and are no longer able to hold the kneecap in its correct place.

HOW TO KNOW IF YOUR INJURY IS SERIOUS

Unfortunately, sometimes an injury can be serious. Signs that may suggest a more severe injury include:
- Severe pain which does not subside
- Immediate and profuse swelling
- Deformity of the affected part
- Inability to take weight on the affected part
- Extreme loss of function
- Guarding (a tensing of the muscles to guard the injured area) or unusual or false motion
- Noises (grating or cracking) at injury site

If you have any of the above, it is recommended you seek urgent medical advice.

TREATMENT
- Use the P.R.I.C.E. principles as initial treatment for the pain and inflammation (see page 68).
- Keep the quads well developed by following a strength-training programme (see pages 166–167).
- Run in suitable footwear that provides you with the necessary support.

SHIN SPLINTS

Shin splints is a pretty general term given to any pain that arises on the front of the lower leg – the medial border of the tibia (inside of the shin) – or simply to describe shin pain in general. It is a common injury in runners, especially when increasing training load or distance, and can have devastating consequences to a training plan. At its worst it can limit day-to-day activity as well as training.

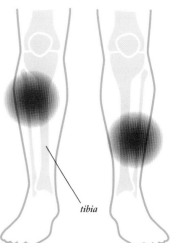

tibia

SYMPTOMS
• **Aches and pains running down the shins**

CAUSES
Shin splints are usually a result of inflammation of the muscles in the lower leg due to the pulling of the tibialis anterior or soleus muscles at the place where they attach to the shin bone. Without the muscle support, undue stress is placed upon the shin bone itself. In extreme cases this can lead to stress fractures (tiny cracks and minute fragmentations) in the shin bone itself – a source of chronic pain.

Shin splints can be caused by poor training techniques. It is a very common injury for new runners, as the activity will not develop the front and inside of the leg as fast as it develops the calf muscles, with the result that the medial muscles and tendons become overworked. Pronated (flat) feet, incorrect choice of footwear type or poor flexibility can also lead to shin splints.

TREATMENT
For something that can develop into such a serious debilitating injury, shin splints are relatively easy to cure if addressed in the early stages. However, of all of the over-use running injuries, this unfortunately is one that people tend to have recurrent problems with, and the only way to stop this is to continue to work on preventative measures.

• Use the P.R.I.C.E. principles as initial treatment (see page 68).
• Massage will help to improve this problem. You can use a foam roller to achieve this effect at home (see page 76).
• Make certain you are running with the correct shoe for your foot type.
• Stretch thoroughly before and after exercise, giving particular attention to the calf muscles (see pages 52–57).
• Progress your distances with a structured and gradual plan. Cut back on duration and build back up slowly if necessary.
• Improving your running technique (see pages 26–35) will help not only to treat but also prevent this problem.

FOAM ROLLING

A foam roller is a cylindrical piece of hard cell foam. It is used for self-massage by applying pressure to the desired area of the body in long, sweeping movements or to "release" knots in the muscle by applying sustained pressure over a particular tender area. The roller helps to provide what is known as "myofascial release", a technique that massage therapists use to increase blood flow and relax over-tight muscles. A foam roller is an extremely useful tool and highly recommended for all runners – it helps to aid recovery and can prevent and treat injury.

When choosing to buy a roller you will find that they come in a variety of shapes and sizes. You will probably find a longer, thicker roller around 90 centimetres long by 15 centimetres in diameter (exact dimensions will vary depending on make) to be most versatile. You will also notice that rollers vary in density; if you are new to using the roller, or if you have particularly tight or tender muscles, you will most likely find a softer roller to be most comfortable to use. However, as you get accustomed to using a foam roller you will probably find one with a firmer density to be more beneficial.

One of the roller's great advantages is its versatility. It can be used either as part of your warm-up or cool-down routines or independently of exercise. Focus on the muscles or areas of the body that you find ache or are particular tight after training. While the roller can be used on almost any muscle or area of the body, a thorough foam-rolling routine for runners should include all the options illustrated on the following pages.

When using the roller over the muscles, roll along the length of the muscle using long sweeping movements. Aim to perform 10–20 repetitions of this movement for each muscle. If you are aware of any particularly tight or tender areas, slow the movement down and apply direct pressure for up to 30 seconds – you should feel the tension/tenderness start to ease off.

It isn't unusual to find that the roller can initially be quite painful to use. Don't let this put you off, as the discomfort will ease with practice.

MIDDLE BACK

Focus on the area between the top and bottom of the shoulder blades. Breathe out as you lean back over the roller and move the roller up and down 2–3 times to target the various parts of the back. This movement helps to expand the chest and extend the spine.

GLUTES

Sit on the roller and lean your body weight to one side. Roll backwards and forwards along the buttock muscle. You might find some areas that are more tender than others – focus on these points. Repeat for the other side.

ITB

Lie on your side with the roller between your outer thigh and the floor. Use your body weight to apply pressure to the outer thigh from just above the knee to the top of the hip. Roll up and down before repeating on the other side.

HAMSTRINGS

Sit down on the roller with your bodyweight on the back of the leg underneath the knee. Roll up to the buttock and back down to the knee a few times before repeating on the other leg.

QUADS
Lie face down with the roller between the front of your thigh and the floor. Use your bodyweight to roll forwards and backwards along the front of the thigh between the hip and the knee. Repeat on the other leg.

CALVES
Place the roller between the calf muscle and the floor. Roll backwards and forwards between the ankle and the back of the knee. Repeat on the other leg.

THE
PROGRAMMES

HOW TO USE THE PROGRAMMES

This book contains a plethora of information, techniques and programmes to ensure that you fulfil your goals and your potential.

There are 5 different distance running programmes that are available to follow, from a 5K run right through to running an ultra distance event, meaning that there is something here to suit everybody. Within each of the programmes there is a choice of levels to suit running experience and fitness, which allows you to adapt the routine to your own personal needs. Two programmes have been given for 5K and 10K distances – one routine for the runner beginning to run at this distance and another for the experienced runner aiming to record a "personal best" (or PB) over the same length. Half-marathon and marathon training distances have been given three routines – a beginner's, a "fast" routine for intermediates and a PB, while only one routine has been given for ultra-distance running, which has been designed for experienced runners to use.

REST UP

Follow the plan that suits your goal and try to stick to it rigidly. Equally, don't get carried away in the potential euphoria of good training and do too much! Rest days are in the plan for a reason; enjoy the break and come back to your training refreshed and raring to go.

Within each programme you will see the weekly layout of training outlined that you are to complete. There is space to make some simple notes on each page to remind you about speeds, duration, routes or anything else that you find to be important to you during the work in that week. This is important as it will act not only as a great reference point for future training routines, but also for comparison during the same routine.

At the start of each routine there are some target times for the distance ahead which should help give you a general idea of the time you should be looking to finish the distance in. Use these to gauge a target time or finishing goal that is specific for you, write it down and refer back to it as you train. Try do this each time you begin a new routine – it is a really powerful way of keeping you focused on every session and every performance. Ineed your primary goal doesn't have to be time-related – it might just be completing a race, or doing it for charity. Just remember that whatever you choose needs to be your primary motivation and you need to keep on reminding yourself of it as often as possible.

SCHEDULE ROTATION

The training week schedules outlined here work on the assumption that most people will have more time to complete a longer run and to get to a park or an off-road route at the weekend. The schedules can, however, be rotated to make any day the start – just pick which day to begin on and off you go!

NON-RUNNING PROGRAMMES

Each routine will give you a session to complete that may be running-, resistance- or drill-based. The four resistance programmes featured within the programmes are detailed on pages 166–167, while the track-based drill programmes are explained in full on pages 160–163.

WARMING UP AND COOLING DOWN

As I've mentioned before, warming up and cooling down are both crucial for injury prevention and for maximising performance. The stretches on pages 52–57 should be completed both before and after any running session. The mobility drills detailed on pages 58–61 should be completed after your initial warm-up stretches but before you begin your run. Where a warm-up or cool-down is specified within a run, this indicates a gentle jog or slow start off or finish to the session at minimal intensity.

MAXIMUM HEART RATE (MHR)

Your maximum heart rate (MHR) is the highest number of times your heart will beat per minute. To get the absolute maximum from your running, the programmes may specify that you run within a certain percentage of this maximum rate. Calculate this by first determining your maximum heart rate: assume that your MHR when you are born is 220 and that every year your heart rate reduces by one, so your MHR = 220 minus your age. So, if you are 40, your MHR is 180 beats per minute (BPM).

Although you can work out your heart rate by stopping and taking your pulse, when running it is easiest to keep track of your heart rate by wearing a heart-rate monitor (see page 45). These can be set to beep if you stray outside a certain heart-rate band, keeping you working at the optimal heart rate for each run. The heart-rate chart shows the percentage of MHR for different age groups in average bpm. Use it to find your optimum training zone.

AGE	70% MHR	75% MHR	80% MHR	85% MHR	90% MHR
18–25	139	149	159	169	179
26–30	134	144	153	163	172
31–36	130	140	149	158	168
37–42	126	135	144	153	162
43–50	121	129	138	147	155
51–58	116	124	133	141	149
59–65	110	118	126	134	142
66+	106	114	121	129	136

This is the entry point to running for most people. That doesn't mean it is easy; it simply means it is one of the shortest distance events that you will find. How hard it is depends upon how hard you push and how fit you are. How much of a success it is depends upon your expectation management and your purpose for doing the run!

If you are truly running just to complete the distance, then time is immaterial and the accomplishment itself will make you feel elated. If you are experienced and fired up, you might have a goal of smashing through the 20-minute barrier and seeing just what your body can achieve.

While this is the shortest of the distances covered here, it still deserves treating with respect. Sounding short does not make it short! It is still 5K, or just over 3 miles, so it really isn't easy. There are two training plans given here set over an eight-week period – one for first-time runners and one for those who are training to pull out a new "personal best".

Both should be followed in a disciplined manner to ensure that you are successful and that you enjoy the experience. There's nothing worse than getting to the start line and feeling unsure about whether you are able to complete the distance – it will make your legs feel weak and your mind become uncertain.

Follow the plan that suits your goal and try to stick to it rigidly. Equally, don't get carried away if your training is going really well and end up doing too much! Rest days are in the plan for a reason. Enjoy them before coming back refreshed and ready to train hard.

TIME EXPECTATIONS

Beginner	*30–36 mins*
Intermediate	*24–29 mins*
Advanced	*20–23 mins*
High Level	*under 20 mins*

5K

MONDAY	REST	REST
	PB 20-min run (constant pace) at 75% MHR.	PB As above.
TUESDAY	**STEADY RUN/WALK** Getting time on your feet. Run or walk (if necessary) at a pace you can still chat. **20 mins** — *Constant pace*	**STEADY RUN/WALK** **20 mins** — *Constant pace* **Resistance B1**
	PB 20-min run (constant pace) at 70% MHR; Resistance A1.	PB 30-min run (constant pace) at 75% MHR; Resistance A2.
WEDNESDAY	REST	REST
	PB As above.	PB As above.
THURSDAY	**STEADY RUN/WALK** **20 mins** — *Constant pace* **Resistance B1**	**STEADY RUN/WALK** **20 mins** — *Constant pace*
	PB 30-min run (constant pace) at 75% MHR; Resistance A2.	PB 8 x 90 sec intervals at 80% MHR with 60 secs rest between each.
FRIDAY	REST	REST
	PB As above.	PB As above.
SATURDAY	**LONG WALK** **60 mins** — *Brisk walk* **Resistance B2**	**LONG WALK** **60 mins** — *Brisk walk* **Resistance B2**
	PB 8 x 90 sec intervals at 80% MHR with 60 secs rest between each.	PB 35-min easy run (constant pace) at 70–75% MHR; Resistance A2.
SUNDAY	**LONG SLOW DISTANCE RUN** Start building the distance you can run, though walk if necessary. **20 mins** — *Constant easy pace*	**LONG SLOW DISTANCE RUN** **25 mins** — *Constant easy pace*
	PB 30-min easy run (constant pace) at 70% MHR.	PB 20-min fartlek session A (track).

REST

REST

PB As above.

PB As above.

STEADY RUN/WALK

20 mins *Constant pace*

Resistance B1

STEADY RUN

20 mins *Constant pace*

Resistance B2

PB 30-min run (constant pace) at 75% MHR;
Resistance A1.

PB 40-min easy run (constant pace) at 70–75%
MHR.

REST

REST

PB As above.

PB As above.

STEADY RUN/WALK

25 mins *Constant pace*

Resistance B2

STEADY RUN

20 mins *Constant pace*

Resistance B1

PB 10 x intervals of 1 min at 75% MHR/1
min at slow jog pace (20 mins total).

PB On a 150m hill, run 10 hills. Walk back to
recover between each. Resistance A2.

REST

REST

PB As above.

PB 20-min run (constant pace) at 75%
MHR.

LONG WALK

60 mins *Brisk walk*

Resistance B1

LONG WALK

60 mins *Brisk walk*

Resistance B2

PB 40-min long run (constant pace) at 70–75%
MHR.

PB Resistance A1.

LONG SLOW DISTANCE RUN

30 mins *Constant easy pace*

LONG SLOW DISTANCE RUN

25 mins *Constant easy pace*

PB 5K run at 70–75% MHR; Resistance A2.

PB 10 mins at 85% MHR/5 mins at 70%
MHR/10 mins at 85% MHR (25 mins total).

Don't worry about walking part of the distance of your steady run when starting out. It's better to do this than to make the mistake of doing too much too soon.

MONDAY	REST	REST
	PB As above.	PB As above.
TUESDAY	**STEADY RUN** **20 mins** *Constant pace* **Resistance B2**	**STEADY RUN** **25 mins** *Constant pace* **Resistance B2**
	PB 30-min run (constant pace) at 75% MHR; Resistance A2.	PB 20-min run (constant pace) at 80% MHR.
WEDNESDAY	REST	REST
	PB As above.	PB Resistance A2.
THURSDAY	**INTERVALS** **25 mins (total)** *10 mins warm-up, then 10 x intervals of 30 secs at fast pace/60 secs easy pace.*	**INTERVALS** **25 mins (total)** *10 mins warm-up, then 10 x intervals of 30 secs at fast pace/60 secs easy pace.*
	PB Threshold run session (track).	PB On a 200m hill, run 8–10 hills. Jog back to recover between each.
FRIDAY	REST	REST
	PB As above.	PB As above.
SATURDAY	**LONG WALK** **60 mins** *Brisk walk* **Resistance B1**	**LONG WALK** **60 mins** *Brisk walk* **Resistance B1**
	PB 8k run at 75% MHR; Resistance A2.	PB 20-min run (constant pace) at 75% MHR; Resistance A1.
SUNDAY	**LONG SLOW DISTANCE RUN** **30 mins** *Constant easy pace*	**LONG SLOW DISTANCE RUN** **35 mins** *Constant easy pace*
	PB 20-min easy run (constant pace) at 70–75% MHR; Resistance A1.	PB 5k run at 80% MHR.

REST

REST

PB As above.

PB As above.

STEADY RUN

STEADY RUN

25 mins   *Constant pace*

20 mins   *Constant pace*

Resistance B2

PB Tempo run session (track); Resistance A2.

PB 20-min easy run (constant pace).

REST

REST

PB As above.

PB As above.

INTERVALS

INTERVALS

30 mins total

20 mins total

10 mins warm-up, then 7 x intervals of 30 secs at fast pace/60 secs easy pace. Cool down for remainder.

10 mins warm-up, then 5 x intervals of 30 secs at fast pace/60 secs easy pace. Cool down for remainder.

PB 30-min run (constant pace) at 75% MHR.

PB 10 mins at 75% MHR/ 3 mins at 85% MHR/7 mins at 70–75% MHR (20 mins total).

REST

REST

PB 25-min run (constant pace) at 85% MHR; Resistance A1.

PB As above.

LONG WALK

REST

60 mins   *Brisk walk*

Resistance B1

PB Striding out session (track).

PB As above.

LONG SLOW DISTANCE RUN

40 mins   *Constant easy pace*

PB 20-min run (constant pace) at 85% MHR; Resistance A2.

This is my personal favourite distance to run. It is long enough to require some real endurance, yet short enough to put some real speed into the equation. For me, as an ex-sprinter, it is the perfect distance challenge. For seasoned marathon runners it is a short run to let the legs recover from the really long stuff. As always, it is all about how hard you push that determines the difficulty.

For a beginner this distance can be challenging. At almost six and a half miles it is not short and will definitely require some serious training if you intend to avoid discomfort and enjoy the race.

This distance, in terms of the time it takes to complete, is outside most people's normal cardiovascular workout range. Many workouts only include cardio periods of 20–40 minutes, so doing a run that will take even the fitter individuals 35–45 minutes to finish is bound to be a serious test of your fitness.

While you will hear many people talk about having completed multiple half marathons and marathons, 10K is the distance at which you become a serious distance runner. For the beginner, the distance is a real achievement and is something that you will complete with an enormous sense of pride. Hopefully, if you follow the plan thoroughly, you will also surprise yourself at how much more achievable the distance proved than you first imagined.

For the advanced runner I have included a personal best plan here that aims to get the maximum speed and endurance from your legs, and the optimum level of cardiovascular conditioning for your heart. As you will know from running these before, the last 3K needs you to feel as fresh and strong as possible and it is the track sessions, hill training and resistance work detailed that will give you the ability to push that extra 20 or 30%, confident in the knowledge that you won't run out of gas. At the risk of sounding like a broken record, remember also that rest days are in the plan for a reason – enjoy them!

TIME EXPECTATIONS

Beginner	*56–70 mins*
Intermediate	*45–55 mins*
Advanced	*38–44 mins*
High Level	*under 38 mins*

	1	2
MONDAY	REST	REST
	PB 30-min run (constant pace) at 75% MHR.	PB As above.
TUESDAY	**STEADY RUN/WALK** Getting time on your feet. Run or walk (if necessary) at a pace at which you can still chat. **20 mins** _Constant pace_ **Resistance B1**	**STEADY RUN/WALK** **25 mins** _Constant pace_ **Resistance B1**
	PB REST	PB 25-min run (constant pace) at 75% MHR; Resistance A2.
WEDNESDAY	**INTERVALS** **30 mins (total)** _5 mins warm-up, then 10 x intervals of 60 secs at brisk run/60 secs easy pace. 5 mins cool-down to finish._	**INTERVALS** **20 mins (total)** _5 mins warm-up, then 5 x intervals of 60 secs at brisk run/60 secs walk. 5 mins cool-down to finish._
	PB Intervals as above; Resistance A1.	PB 5 mins warm-up, then 10 x intervals of 90 secs brisk run/60 secs walk. 5 mins cool-down to finish.
THURSDAY	REST	REST
	PB As above.	PB Resistance A1.
FRIDAY	**TEMPO RUN** **20 mins (total)** _5 mins easy pace, followed by 10 mins faster pace, then 5 mins easy pace to finish._ **Resistance B2**	**TEMPO RUN** **20 mins (total)** _5 mins easy pace, followed by 10 mins faster pace, then 5 mins easy pace to finish._ **Resistance B2**
	PB 30-min run (constant pace) at 75% MHR; Resistance A2.	PB 40-min run (constant pace) at 75% MHR; Resistance A2.
SATURDAY	REST	REST
	PB As above.	PB As above.
SUNDAY	**LONG SLOW DISTANCE RUN** Start to build the distance covered in one run. Run at an easy pace at which you can chat. **30 mins** _Constant easy pace_	**LONG SLOW DISTANCE RUN** **40 mins** _Constant easy pace_
	PB 40-min easy run (constant pace) at 70% MHR; Resistance A2.	PB 10 mins at 70% MHR then 5 mins at 85% MHR. Repeat 3 times.

REST	REST
PB As above.	PB 25-min slow run (constant pace) at 75% MHR; Resistance A2.
STEADY RUN/WALK **30 mins** *Constant pace* **Resistance B1**	**STEADY RUN/WALK** **25 mins** *Constant pace* **Resistance B1**
PB 25-min run (constant pace) at 75% MHR; Resistance A1.	PB REST
INTERVALS **20 mins (total)** *5 mins warm-up, then 5 x intervals of 60 secs at brisk run/60 secs walk. 5 mins cool-down to finish.*	**INTERVALS** **20 mins (total)** *5 mins warm-up, then 5 x intervals of 60 secs brisk run/60 secs jog. 5 mins cool-down to finish.*
PB Fartlek session B (track)	PB Maximum intensity intervals session B (track); Resistance A1.
REST	REST
PB Resistance A2.	PB As above.
TEMPO RUN **22 mins (total)** *5 mins easy pace, followed by 12 mins faster pace, then 5 mins easy pace to finish.* **Resistance B2**	**TEMPO RUN** **20 mins (total)** *5 mins easy pace, followed by 10 mins faster pace, then 5 mins easy pace to finish.* **Resistance B2**
PB As above.	PB 30-min run (constant pace) at 75% MHR; Resistance A2.
REST	REST
PB As above.	PB As above.
LONG SLOW DISTANCE RUN **50 mins** **Constant easy pace**	**LONG SLOW DISTANCE RUN** **45 mins** **Constant easy pace**
PB 10K at 70–75% MHR; Resistance A1.	PB 12K at 70% MHR.

Tempo runs are great for building speed and stamina. The faster-paced sections should be at "controlled discomfort" – you should be able to speak a few words, but not whole sentences as you do them.

	5	6
MONDAY	REST	REST
	PB As above.	PB As above.
TUESDAY	**STEADY RUN** Getting time on your feet. Run at a pace you can still chat. **35 mins** *Constant pace* **Resistance B1**	**STEADY RUN** **40 mins** *Constant pace*
	PB 25-min fast run (constant pace) at 80% MHR; Resistance A2	PB Threshold runs session (track)
WEDNESDAY	**INTERVALS** **26 mins (total)** *5 mins warm up, then 8 x intervals of 60 secs brisk run/60 secs jog. 5 mins cool-down to finish.*	**INTERVALS** **30 mins (total)** *10 mins warm-up, then 6 x intervals of 90 secs brisk run/60 secs jog. 5 mins cool-down to finish.* **Resistance B1**
	PB Striding out session (track).	PB 30-min run (constant pace) at 75% MHR; Resistance A1.
THURSDAY	REST	REST
	PB 30-min fast run at 80% MHR; Resistance A1.	PB As above.
FRIDAY	**TEMPO RUN** **32 mins (total)** *10 mins easy pace, followed by 12 mins faster pace, then 10 mins easy pace to finish.* **Resistance B2**	**TEMPO RUN** **41 mins (total)** *10 mins easy pace/8 mins faster pace/5 mins easy/8 mins faster/10 mins easy pace to finish.* **Resistance B1**
	PB REST	PB As above.
SATURDAY	REST	REST
	PB On a 150m hill, run 10–12 hills. Walk back to recover between each. Resistance A2.	PB 10K at 80% MHR.
SUNDAY	**LONG SLOW DISTANCE RUN** Building the distance now, you should be covering 8–10K. **55 mins** *Constant easy pace*	**LONG SLOW DISTANCE RUN** **60 mins** *Constant easy pace*
	PB 60-min easy run (constant pace) at 70–75% MHR.	PB Striding out session (track).

REST

REST

PB As above.

PB 30-min easy run (constant pace).

STEADY RUN

35 mins   *Constant pace*

Resistance B1

STEADY RUN

This run should feel easy and enjoyable.

30 mins   *Constant pace*

PB 45–50-min run (constant pace) at 75% MHR; Resistance A2.

PB REST

INTERVALS

30 mins

5 mins warm-up, then 8 x intervals of 90 secs brisk run/60 secs jog. 5 mins cool-down to finish.

INTERVALS

25 mins

10 mins warm-up, then 5 x intervals of 30 secs sprint/30 secs jog. 10 mins cool-down to finish.

PB Resistance A1.

PB 25-min steady run at 80% MHR.

REST

REST

PB 5 mins easy pace/10 mins faster/5 mins easy/8 mins faster/4 mins easy/6 mins faster/2 mins easy to finish.

PB As above.

TEMPO RUN

35 mins (total)

5 mins easy pace/10 mins faster/5 mins easy/10 mins faster/5 mins easy to finish.

Resistance B2

EASY RUN

Stretch your legs out and take it easy. This may feel hard, but it's just nerves. You are ready to race.

20 mins   *Constant pace*

PB Resisance A1.

PB As above.

REST

REST

PB 7.5K at 80% MHR; Resistance A1.

PB As above.

LONG SLOW DISTANCE RUN

50 mins   *Constant easy pace*

RACE DAY

You've made it, only 10K to go. Enjoy it, you've worked hard!

PB REST

If you are a first-timer you will be viewing this distance with the same anticipation, nervousness and excitement as you might a marathon. This is entirely appropriate – at 21K, or around 13 miles, this is truly a long distance event! It is a run that requires thorough preparation, pace discipline, a hydration strategy and some good mental planning to get through it, whether you're running for the first time or for a best time.

There are three plans detailed here for this distance, as I have added an extra "fast" or intermediate level to the beginner and personal best programmes. The reason for this is that, with the greater distance involved, fitness levels and experience start to make a real difference to what you can expect to achieve. While at 5 or 10K anyone who has perhaps completed one of the runs already or just feels confident can push hard on their first go; with a half marathon this is not the case. As such, the intermediate and personal best programmes here should only be attempted by those who have a good base level of fitness and some previous experience of running.

At an intermediate level, pacing strategy is vital, and your training runs are going to be key to understanding just how your body responds when pushed for more than 60 to 75 minutes. It is at this point that hydration and nutrition levels become a major factor, so practice during training will be fundamental to your success. For the advanced runner, this event takes real determination to push hard as fatigue sets in. With all of the programmes your physical strength is going to be important when maintaining your running posture and form as you become tired. The resistance training programmes will help to develop this base and allow you to focus on your cardiovascular performance when you need to.

For most people who run marathons, the half marathon is a great event to run in to get used to the feeling of running a long distance with a large group of people, and forms an integral part of the marathon training programme. It is a great distance and, when you finish, you will really deserve the medal!

TIME EXPECTATIONS

Beginner	*2 hours–2 hours 30 mins*
Intermediate	*1 hour 40 mins–1 hour 59 mins*
Advanced	*1 hour 25 mins–1 hour 39 mins*
High Level	*under 1 hour 25 mins*

HALF
MARATHON

	1	2
MONDAY	REST	REST
TUESDAY	**STEADY RUN/WALK** Getting time on your feet. Run or walk (if necessary) at a pace you can still chat. **20 mins** *Constant pace*	**STEADY RUN/WALK** **20 mins** *Constant pace* **Resistance B1**
WEDNESDAY	**INTERVAL TRAINING** It's early days, but we're laying the ground work for gaining some speed. **20 mins (total)** *5 mins warm-up, then 5 x intervals of 60 secs at a brisk run/60 secs at an easy pace. 5 mins cool-down to finish.* **Resistance B1**	**INTERVAL TRAINING** **20 mins (total)** *5 mins warm-up, then 5 x intervals of 60 secs at a brisk run/60 secs at an easy pace. 5 mins cool-down to finish.*
THURSDAY	REST	REST
FRIDAY	**TEMPO RUN** Learn how it feels to run at different paces. **20 mins (total)** *5 mins easy pace, followed by 10 mins faster pace, then 5 mins easy pace to finish.* **Resistance B2**	**TEMPO RUN** **20 mins (total)** *5 mins easy pace, followed by 10 mins faster pace, then 5 mins easy pace to finish.* **Resistance B2**
SATURDAY	REST	REST
SUNDAY	**LONG SLOW DISTANCE RUN** Starting to build distance covered in one run. Run at an easy pace at which you can chat. **30 mins** *Constant easy pace*	**LONG SLOW DISTANCE RUN** **40 mins** *Constant easy pace*

REST

STEADY RUN/WALK

25 mins   *Constant pace*

Resistance B1

INTERVAL TRAINING
The "brisk" intervals here should feel hard – you should not be able to talk while doing them. Slow right down for the jog to get your breath back.

20 mins (total)

5 mins warm-up, then 5 x intervals of 60 secs at a brisk run/60 secs at an easy jog. 5 mins cool-down finish.

REST

TEMPO RUN
The faster pace section here is best described as "controlled discomfort". You should be able to speak only a few words as you do it.
22 mins (total)

5 mins easy pace, followed by 12 mins faster pace, then 5 mins easy pace to finish.
Resistance B2

REST

LONG SLOW DISTANCE RUN

50 mins   *Constant easy pace*

TOP 10 RUNNING TIPS

At the Matt Roberts Running Clinic I work with runners of all levels of ability all of the time. While each of them has to be guided and pushed through the appropriate individual routines for their needs, they have all benefited from some helpful advice which can make *everyone's* running easier and more fun. The following collection of running tips – as relayed through the experiences of some of my trainees – will help to make your running as enjoyable as possible.

TOP TIP # 1
SET YOURSELF GOALS

"I find that setting clear goals is the best way to keep myself running. Whenever I run a race, my goal is always to complete the distance and do my best, while trying to encourage as many people as possible to start running along the way!"

NELL MCANDREW

	4	5
MONDAY	REST	REST
TUESDAY	**STEADY RUN/WALK** **20 mins** *Constant pace* **Resistance B1**	**STEADY RUN** **30 mins** *Constant pace* **Resistance B1**
WEDNESDAY	**INTERVAL TRAINING** **20 mins (total)** *5 mins warm-up, then 5 x intervals of 60 secs at a brisk run/60 secs at an easy jog. 5 mins cool-down to finish.*	**INTERVAL TRAINING** **26 mins** *5 mins warm-up, then 8 x intervals of 60 secs at a brisk run/60 secs at an easy jog. 5 mins cool-down to finish.*
THURSDAY	REST	REST
FRIDAY	**TEMPO RUN** **20 mins (total)** *5 mins easy pace, followed by 10 mins faster pace, then 5 mins easy pace to finish.* **Resistance B2**	**TEMPO RUN** **22 mins (total)** *5 mins easy pace, followed by 12 mins faster pace, then 5 mins easy pace to finish.* **Resistance B2**
SATURDAY	REST	REST
SUNDAY	**LONG SLOW DISTANCE RUN** **45 mins** *Constant easy pace*	**LONG SLOW DISTANCE RUN** **55 mins** *Constant easy pace*

REST

STEADY RUN

30 mins *Constant pace*

Resistance B1

INTERVAL TRAINING

25 mins (total)

5 mins warm-up, then 6 x intervals of 90 secs at a brisk run/60 secs at an easy jog. 5 mins cool-down to finish.

REST

TEMPO RUN

31 mins (total)

5 mins easy pace/8 mins faster/5 mins easy/8 mins faster/5 mins easy to finish.

Resistance B1

REST

LONG SLOW DISTANCE RUN

60 mins *Constant easy pace*

TOP TIP # 2
FOLLOW YOUR PLAN

"At first glance, my training programme for the marathon looked really daunting. While it did get tougher as time went on, the idea behind it was that your strength and stamina increase as you train, so the extra work didn't come as too much of a shock to the system!"

JENNI FALCONER

TOP TIP # 3
DRINK FOR VICTORY

"Post-run nutrition is really important. I often have a big glass of milk as soon as I can after a run. After this year's marathon I made sure I had a recovery drink packed in my bag for after the run. As you don't usually want to eat straight away, it's a great way to refuel your body."

NELL MCANDREW

	7	**8**
MONDAY	REST	REST
TUESDAY	**STEADY RUN** **35 mins** *Constant pace* **Resistance B2**	**STEADY RUN** **25 mins** *Constant pace* **Resistance B2**
WEDNESDAY	**INTERVAL TRAINING** **30 mins (total)** *5 mins warm-up, then 8 x intervals of 90 secs at a brisk run/60 secs at a jog. 5 mins cool-down to finish.*	**INTERVAL TRAINING** We're now throwing in a few 30-second sprints for some serious speed and fun. Stride out and keep your shoulders relaxed. **25 mins (total)** *10 mins warm-up, then 5 x 30 secs sprint/30 secs at a brisk jog. 10 mins cool-down to finish.*
THURSDAY	REST	REST
FRIDAY	**TEMPO RUN** **35 mins (total)** *5 mins easy pace/10 mins faster/5 mins easy/10 mins faster/5 mins easy to finish.* **Resistance B1**	**TEMPO RUN** **31 mins (total)** *5 mins easy pace/8 mins faster/5 mins easy/8 mins faster/5 mins easy to finish.* **Resistance B1**
SATURDAY	REST	REST
SUNDAY	**LONG SLOW DISTANCE RUN** **65 mins** *Constant easy pace*	**LONG SLOW DISTANCE RUN** **55 mins** *Constant easy pace*

Resistance B2

STEADY RUN

40 mins — *Constant pace*

INTERVAL TRAINING

30 mins (total)

5 mins warm-up, then 8 x 90 secs brisk run/60 secs jog. 5 mins cool-down to finish.

Resistance B1

REST

TEMPO RUN

39 mins (total)

5 mins easy pace/12 mins faster/ 5 mins easy/12 mins faster/5 mins easy pace to finish.

Resistance B2

REST

LONG SLOW DISTANCE RUN

70 mins — *Constant easy pace*

TOP TIP # 4
VARY YOUR ROUTES

"When I started training for the marathon, I found that some of the longer runs could feel quite boring and lonely, but varying my routes helped break up the sessions and made them go quicker."

VICKY ELLISON

TOP TIP # 5
CROSS-TRAIN FOR SUCCESS

"When I struggle with my motivation during training, I treat myself to some personal training sessions. It's always good to learn new exercises and new ways to train. It's great to just turn up and get stuck in, and it's also always more difficult to give in when someone is training with you!"

NELL MCANDREW

	10	**11**
MONDAY	Resistance B1	REST
TUESDAY	**STEADY RUN** **45 mins** *Constant pace*	**STEADY RUN** **50 mins** *Constant pace*
WEDNESDAY	**HILL TRAINING** To build leg strength, introduce some hills into your interval training. Push on the uphill and make the downhill an easy jog. **32 mins (total)** *10 mins warm-up then, on a 200m hill, run 6 hills. Jog back to recover between each. 10 mins cool-down to finish.* **Resistance B2**	**INTERVAL TRAINING** **34 mins (total)** *5 mins warm-up then 8 x 2 mins brisk run/60 secs jog. 5 mins cool-down to finish.* **Resistance B1**
THURSDAY	REST	REST
FRIDAY	**TEMPO RUN** **45 mins (total)** *5 mins easy pace/15 mins faster/5 mins easy/15 mins faster/5 mins easy to finish.* **Resistance B1**	**PACING RUN** Pick an out and back route. Run a steady pace for the outbound leg and try to keep same pace for return leg, i.e. get back to the start. **45 mins (total)** *20 mins out at a steady pace followed by 20 mins back to start at the same pace. 5 mins easy cool-down to finish.* **Resistance B2**
SATURDAY	REST	REST
SUNDAY	**LONG SLOW DISTANCE RUN** **80 mins** *Constant easy pace*	**LONG SLOW DISTANCE RUN** **90 mins** *Constant easy pace*

REST

STEADY RUN

| 45 mins | Constant pace |

Resistance B1

INTERVAL TRAINING

30 mins (total)

10 mins warm-up then 10 x 30 secs sprint/30 secs jog. 10 mins cool-down to finish.

Resistance B2

STEADY RUN

Prior to a race you need to ease back so you are fresh for the race. Steady run only today.

| 30 mins | Constant pace |

Resistance B1

REST

PRACTICE RACE

Find a 10K race to enter (or run 10K at race pace).

| 50–60 mins | Race pace |

TOP TIP # 5
DON'T FORGET THE GYM

"Before I started training with Matt I never appreciated how crucial weight training sessions were to my running; your stamina is wholly affected by your strength. If you've done the training then, even when you're tired, your legs will still have the strength to carry you and your arms will still power you along!"

JENNI FALCONER

TOP TIP # 6
VARY YOUR RUNNING

"You can never, ever underestimate the importance of varying your runs, in particular including sessions of hill training to really build strength and stamina. I have noticed a massive difference in my running since including hill sessions in my training. Once you've done a hill session, running on the flat feels easy."

NELL MCANDREW

	13	14
MONDAY	Resistance B1	Resistance B1
TUESDAY	**STEADY RUN** 55 mins *Constant pace*	**STEADY RUN** 60 mins *Constant pace*
WEDNESDAY	**INTERVAL TRAINING** The fast intervals here should be at your 10K pace or about 80% effort. Slow right down for the jog to get your breath back. **34 mins (total)** *5 mins warm-up then 6 x 3 mins fast run/1 min jog. 5 mins cool-down to finish.* **Resistance B2**	**HILL TRAINING** **36 mins (total)** *10 mins warm-up then, on a 200m hill, run 8 hills. Jog back to recover between each. 10 mins cool-down to finish.* **Resistance B2**
THURSDAY	REST	REST
FRIDAY	**TEMPO RUN** **51 mins (total)** *5 mins easy pace/18 mins faster/5 mins easy/18 mins faster/5 mins easy to finish.*	**TEMPO RUN** **55 mins (total)** *5 mins easy pace/20 mins faster/ 5 mins easy/20 mins faster/5 mins easy to finish.*
SATURDAY	REST	REST
SUNDAY	**LONG SLOW DISTANCE RUN** 100 mins *Constant easy pace*	**LONG SLOW DISTANCE RUN** 110 mins *Constant easy pace*

15

REST

STEADY RUN

50 mins *Constant pace*

Resistance B1

INTERVAL TRAINING

30 mins (total)

5 mins warm-up then 10 x 90 secs fast/30 secs jog. 5 mins cool-down to finish.

REST

TEMPO RUN

45 mins (total)

5 mins easy pace/15 mins faster/ 5 mins easy/15 mins faster/5 mins easy to finish.

Resistance B2

REST

LONG SLOW DISTANCE RUN
The distance is tapering down before your race. This should feel easy and really comfortable.

75 mins *Constant easy pace*

16

REST

STEADY RUN

30 mins *Constant pace*

INTERVAL TRAINING
A few final sprint blasts to blow those cobwebs away.

25 mins (total)

10 mins warm-up then 5 x 30 secs sprint/30 secs jog. 10 mins cool-down to finish.

REST

EASY RUN
Stretch your legs out and take it easy. This may feel hard, but it's just nerves. You are ready to race.

20 mins (total)

REST

RACE DAY

You've made it, only 13.1 miles to go. Enjoy it, you've worked hard!

	1	**2**
MONDAY	REST	REST
	PB As above.	PB As above.
TUESDAY	**STEADY RUN**	**STEADY RUN**
	30 mins *Constant pace (60% MHR)*	**30 mins** *Constant pace (60% MHR)*
	Resistance A1	**Resistance A2**
	PB As above.	PB As above.
WEDNESDAY	**INTERVAL TRAINING**	**INTERVAL TRAINING**
	25 mins (total)	**28 mins (total)**
	5 mins warm-up, then 5 x intervals of 2 min brisk run at 80% effort/1 min jog or walk. 5 mins cool-down to finish.	*5 mins warm-up, then 6 x intervals of 2 mins brisk run at 80% effort/1 min jog or walk. 5 mins cool-down to finish.*
		Resistance A1
	PB 5 mins warm-up, then 6 x 2 mins run at 80% MHR/1 min jog. 5 mins cool-down to finish.	PB 5 mins warm-up, then 7 x intervals of 2 mins run at 80% MHR/60 secs jog. 5 mins cool-down to finish.
THURSDAY	REST	REST
	PB Resistance A2.	PB Resistance A1.
FRIDAY	**TEMPO RUN**	**TEMPO RUN**
	30 mins (total)	**30 mins (total)**
	5 mins easy pace, followed by 20 mins faster pace at 70% effort, then 5 mins easy pace to finish.	*5 mins easy pace, followed by 20 mins faster pace at 70% effort, then 5 mins easy pace to finish.*
	Resistance A2	**Resistance A2**
	PB Tempo run session (track).	PB Tempo run session (track).
SATURDAY	REST	REST
	PB As above.	PB As above.
SUNDAY	**LONG SLOW DISTANCE RUN**	**LONG SLOW DISTANCE RUN**
	30 mins *Constant easy pace (60% MHR)*	**40 mins** *Constant easy pace (60% MHR)*
	Resistance A1	
	PB Long slow distance run as above; Resistance A1.	PB Long slow distance run as above; Resistance A2.

REST

PB As above.

STEADY RUN

30 mins _Constant pace (60% MHR)_

Resistance A1

PB As above.

INTERVAL TRAINING
34 mins (total)

5 mins warm-up, then 6x intervals of 3 mins brisk run at 80% effort/1 min jog or walk. 5 mins cool-down to finish.

PB Maximum intensity intervals session B (track).

REST

PB Resistance A2.

TEMPO RUN
35 mins (total)

5 mins easy pace/10 mins faster at 70% effort/5 mins easy/10 mins at 70% effort/5 mins easy to finish.

Resistance A2

PB Tempo run of 2 x 5 mins easy pace/15 mins at 70% MHR. 5 mins easy cool-down to finish.

REST

PB As above.

LONG SLOW DISTANCE RUN

50 mins _Constant easy pace (60% MHR)_

PB Long slow distance run as above; Resistance A1.

REST

PB As above.

STEADY RUN

30 mins _Constant pace (60% MHR)_

Resistance A1

PB Steady run as above; Resistance A2.

INTERVAL TRAINING
31 mins (total)

5 mins warm up, then 7 x 2 mins brisk run at 80% effort/1 min jog or walk. 5 mins cool down to finish.

Resistance A2

PB 5 mins warm-up, then 8 x intervals of 2 mins run at 80% MHR/60 secs jog. 5 mins cool-down to finish. Resistance A1.

REST

PB As above.

TEMPO RUN
30 mins (total)

5 mins easy pace, followed by 20 mins faster pace at 70% effort, then 5 mins easy pace to finish.

Resistance A1

PB Tempo run of 5 mins easy pace/30 mins at 70% MHR/5 mins easy cool-down to finish.

REST

PB Resistance A1.

LONG SLOW DISTANCE RUN

45 mins _Constant easy pace (60% MHR)_

PB As above.

A heart-rate monitor is particularly useful for interval training to monitor recovery periods and assess your work rate accurately.

	5	6
MONDAY	REST	REST
	PB Resistance A2.	PB As above.
TUESDAY	**STEADY RUN** **40 mins** *Constant pace (60% MHR)* **Resistance A2** PB Steady run as above; Resistance A1.	**STEADY RUN** **45 mins** *Constant pace (60% MHR)* **Resistance A1** PB Steady run as above; Resistance A2.
WEDNESDAY	**INTERVAL TRAINING** **35 mins (total)** *5 mins warm-up, then 5 x 4 mins at 80% effort/1 min jog or walk. 5 mins cool-down to finish.* **Resistance A1** PB Maximum intensity intervals session A (track). Resistance A2.	**HILL TRAINING** **35 mins (total)** *10 mins warm-up, then, on a 200m hill, run 6 hills. Jog back for 60 secs between each. 10 mins cool-down.* **Resistance A2** PB 10 mins warm-up then, on a 250m hill, run 15 hills at 80% MHR. Jog back to recover between each. 10 mins cool-down to finish.
THURSDAY	REST	REST
	PB As above.	PB As above.
FRIDAY	**TEMPO RUN** **39 mins (total)** *2 x 5 mins easy pace/12 mins faster at 70% effort. 5 mins easy pace to finish.* **Resistance A2** PB Tempo run of 2 x 5 mins easy pace/16 mins at 70% MHR. 5 mins easy cool-down to finish. Resistance A1.	**TEMPO RUN** **45 mins (total)** *2 x 5 mins easy pace/15 mins faster at 70% effort. 5 mins easy pace to finish.* **Resistance A1** PB Tempo run of 2 x 5 mins easy pace/18 mins at 70% MHR. 5 mins easy cool-down to finish.
SATURDAY	REST	REST
	PB As above.	PB As above.
SUNDAY	**LONG SLOW DISTANCE RUN** **55 mins** *Constant easy pace (60% MHR)* PB Long slow distance run as above; Resistance A2.	**LONG SLOW DISTANCE RUN** **60 mins** *Constant easy pace (60% MHR)* PB Long slow distance run as above; Resistance A2.

7	8
Resistance A2	**Resistance A1**
PB REST	PB As above.
STEADY RUN **50 mins** *Constant pace (60% MHR)*	**STEADY RUN** **45 mins** *Constant pace (60% MHR)*
PB Steady run as above; Resistance A1.	PB Steady run as above; Resistance A2.
INTERVAL TRAINING **43 mins (total)** *5 mins warm-up, then 5 x 5 mins at 80% effort/90 secs jog or walk. 5 mins cool-down to finish.* **Resistance A1** PB Maximum intensity intervals session B (track).	**INTERVAL TRAINING** **28 mins (total)** *10 mins warm-up, then 8 x 30 secs sprint at 90% effort/30 secs jog. 10 mins cool-down to finish.* **Resistance A2** PB 10 mins warm up, then 10 x intervals of 30 secs sprint at 90% MHR/30 secs jog. 10 mins cool down to finish.
REST PB Resistance A2.	**REST** PB Resistance A1.
PACING RUN **45 mins (total)** *20 mins out at a steady pace (70% effort) followed by 20 mins back to start at the same pace. 5 mins cool-down.* **Resistance A2** PB As above.	**TEMPO RUN** **45 mins (total)** *2 x 5 mins easy pace/15 mins faster at 70% effort. 5 mins easy pace to finish.* **Resistance A1** PB Tempo run of 2 x 5 mins easy pace/16 mins at 70% MHR. 5 mins easy cool-down to finish.
REST PB Resistance A1.	**REST** PB As above.
LONG SLOW DISTANCE RUN **70 mins** *Constant easy pace (60% MHR)* PB As above.	**LONG SLOW DISTANCE RUN** **60 mins** *Constant easy pace (60% MHR)* PB Long slow distance run as above; Resistance A2.

Be careful of old, long-forgotten injuries when starting to run. If they persist, seek medical advice.

	9	10
MONDAY	**Resistance A1**	REST
	PB As above.	PB Resistance A1.
TUESDAY	**STEADY RUN** **55 mins** *Constant pace (60% MHR)*	**STEADY RUN** **60 mins** *Constant pace (60% MHR)*
	PB As above	PB As above
WEDNESDAY	**HILL TRAINING** **38 mins (total)** *10 mins warm-up then, on a 300m hill, run 6 hills. Jog back down between each. 10 mins cool-down to finish.* **Resistance A2** PB 10 mins warm-up then, on a 300m hill, run 8 hills. Jog back down between each. 10 mins cool-down to finish. Resistance A1.	**INTERVAL PYRAMID RUN** **41 mins (total)** *5 mins warm-up, then 3/5/7/5/3 mins at 80% effort with 90 secs jog between each effort. 5 mins cool-down to finish.* **Resistance A1** PB 5 mins warm-up, then pyramid intervals of 4/6/8/6/4 mins at 85% MHR with 90 secs jog between each run. 5 mins cool-down to finish.
THURSDAY	REST	REST
	PB As above.	PB Resistance A2.
FRIDAY	**TEMPO RUN** **51 mins (total)** *2 x 5 mins easy pace/18 mins faster at 70% effort. 5 mins easy pace to finish.* **Resistance A1** PB Tempo run of 2 x 5 mins easy pace/20 mins at 70% MHR. 5 mins easy cool-down to finish. Resistance A2.	**TEMPO RUN** **55 mins (total)** *5 mins easy pace/20 mins faster at 70% effort/5 mins easy pace/20 mins faster at 70% effort/5 mins easy pace to finish.* PB Tempo run of 2 x 5 mins easy pace/22 mins at 70% MHR. 5 mins easy cool-down to finish.
SATURDAY	REST	**Resistance A2**
	PB As above.	PB REST
SUNDAY	**LONG SLOW DISTANCE RUN** **80 mins** *Easy pace (60% MHR) for 70 mins, then last 10 mins at 70% of target half marathon pace.* PB As above.	**LONG SLOW DISTANCE RUN** **90 mins** *Easy pace (60% MHR) for 75 mins, then last 15 mins at 70% of target half marathon pace.* PB As above.

12

REST

PB Resistance A1.

Resistance A1

PB REST.

STEADY RUN

60 mins *Constant pace (60% MHR)*

PB As above

STEADY RUN

50 mins *Constant pace (60% MHR)*

PB As above

KENYAN HILLS
38 mins (total)

5 mins warm-up, then 4 x run uphill and downhill for 5 mins/2 mins recovery jog. 5 mins cool-down to finish.

Resistance A1

PB Threshold runs session (track).

INTERVAL TRAINING
30 mins (total)

10 mins warm-up, then 10 x 30 secs sprint at 90% effort/30 secs jog. 10 mins cool-down to finish.

PB 10 mins warm-up, then 15 x intervals of 30 secs sprint at 90% MHR/60 secs jog. 10 mins cool-down to finish.

REST

PB Resistance A2.

Resistance A2

PB REST

PACING RUN
55 mins (total)

25 mins out at a steady pace (70% effort) followed by 25 mins back to start at the same pace. 5 mins cool-down.

Resistance A2

PB Pacing run of 30 mins out at a steady pace/30 mins back at same pace. 5 mins easy cool-down to finish.

STEADY RUN

30 mins *Constant pace*

PB 30-min run (constant pace) at 70% MHR. Resistance A2.

REST

PB As above.

REST

PB As above.

LONG SLOW DISTANCE RUN
100 mins

Easy pace (60% MHR) for 80 mins, then last 20 mins at 70% of target half marathon pace.

PB As above.

PRACTICE RACE
50–60 mins *Race pace*

PB As above.

When running Kenyan hills, try to keep a continuous speed going both on the up- and downhill sections for an effective and very different hill workout.

	13	14
MONDAY	REST PB As above.	**Resistance A1** PB As above.
TUESDAY	**STEADY RUN** **60 mins** *Constant pace (60% MHR)* PB As above.	**STEADY RUN** **70 mins** *Constant pace (60% MHR)* PB As above.
WEDNESDAY	**SPRINT FINISH TRAINING** **50 mins (total)** *5 mins warm-up , then 8 x 3 1/2 mins 80% effort/30 secs 95%effort/1 min recovery. 5 mins cool-down to finish.* **Resistance A2** PB Threshold runs session (track).	**KENYAN HILLS** **45 mins (total)** *5 mins warm-up, then 5 x run uphill and downhill for 5 mins/2 mins recovery jog. 5 mins cool-down to finish.* PB Fartlek A session (track).
THURSDAY	REST PB As above.	REST PB Resistance A1.
FRIDAY	**TEMPO RUN** **65 mins (total)** *3 x 5 mins easy pace/15 mins faster at 70% effort. 5 mins easy pace to finish.* PB Tempo run of 3 x 5 mins easy pace/20mins at 70%.	**PACING RUN** **65 mins (total)** *30 mins out at a steady pace (70% effort) followed by 30 mins back to start at the same pace. 5 mins easy cool-down to finish.* PB Pacing run of 35 mins out at a steady pace/35 mins back at same pace. 5 mins easy cool-down to finish.
SATURDAY	REST PB As above.	REST PB As above.
SUNDAY	**LONG SLOW DISTANCE RUN** **110 mins** *Easy pace (60% MHR) for 80 mins, then last 30 mins at 70% of target half marathon pace.* PB As above.	**LONG SLOW DISTANCE RUN** **120 mins** *Easy pace (60% MHR) for 80 mins, then last 40 mins at 70% of target half marathon pace.* PB As above.

Resistance A2

PB Resistance A2.

REST

PB As above.

STEADY RUN

50 mins   *Constant pace (60% MHR)*

PB As above.

STEADY RUN

30 mins   *Constant pace (60% MHR)*

PB As above.

INTERVAL TRAINING

40 mins (total)

10 mins warm-up, then 10 x 90 secs fast run at 85% effort/30 secs recovery jog. 10 mins cool-down to finish.

PB 10 mins warm-up, then 10 x intervals of 90 secs run at 85% MHR/30 secs jog. 10 mins cool-down to finish.

INTERVAL TRAINING

25 mins (total)

10 mins warm-up then 5 x 30 secs sprint/30 secs jog. 10 mins cool-down to finish.

PB 10 mins warm-up, then 5 x intervals of 30 secs sprint at 90% MHR/30 secs jog. 10 mins cool-down to finish.

REST

PB Resistance A1.

REST

PB As above.

TEMPO RUN

45 mins (total)

5 mins easy pace/15 mins faster at 70% effort/5 mins easy/15 mins faster at 70% effort/5 mins easy pace to finish.

PB Tempo run of 2 x 5 mins easy pace/15mins at 70% MHR. 5 mins easy cool-down to finish.

EASY RUN

20 mins   *Constant easy pace*

PB As above.

REST

PB Resistance A2.

REST

PB As above.

LONG SLOW DISTANCE RUN
The distance is coming down before the big day. This should feel really comfortable.

75 mins   *Constant easy pace (60% MHR)*

PB As above.

RACE DAY

You've made it, only 13.1 miles to go. Enjoy it, you've worked hard!

A bit of a blasé attitude to marathon running seems to have developed recently, perhaps because we have come to think of this distance as being quite a high participation event. Don't be fooled, the marathon will feel like every one of its 26.2 miles, and in completing it you are doing something that is genuinely special.

The three levels of training covered here are the same as for the half marathon, and allow the full range of abilities to be catered for. If you are a beginner, training for a marathon can be completed within 16 weeks; however, ideally you should have done some running before this. While it is possible to start running and make the marathon your first goal, I wouldn't recommend it. Beginners, in this context, are beginners to marathon running, not those who are completely new to running in general.

Bear in mind that the progression from a half marathon to a marathon is pretty big! Even if you found running a half marathon to be relatively straightforward, you will almost certainly have moments over this distance that are difficult, no matter how good your preparation. However, with a complete and diligent approach you will be able to ensure that you reach your goal and minimise the chances of anything going wrong.

Completing a marathon will make you feel incredibly proud. You will be filled with a sense of euphoria and downright relief at the same time! Reaching a new best time, or dipping under the obvious "big targets" of 4 hours, 3 1/2hours and 3 hours, should provide you with that extra incentive, if needed.

Understanding your running strategy, hydration, foot gait, pace, eating plan and a host of other factors is vital in marathon running. This really is *not* a run where you can just turn up and hope to somehow wing it.

TIME EXPECTATIONS

Beginner	*4 hours 30 mins–5 hours*
Intermediate	*3 hours 45 mins–3 hours 59 mins*
Advanced	*3 hours–3 hours 43 mins*
High Level	*under 3 hours*

MARATHON

	1	2
MONDAY	REST	REST
TUESDAY	**STEADY RUN/WALK** Getting time on your feet. Run or walk (if necessary) at a pace you can still chat. **Resistance B1** 30 mins *Constant pace*	**STEADY RUN/WALK** 30 mins *Constant pace* **Resistance B1**
WEDNESDAY	**INTERVAL TRAINING** It's early days, but we're laying the ground work for gaining some speed. **30 mins (total)** *10 mins warm-up, then 5 x intervals of 60 secs at a brisk run/60 secs walk. 10 mins cool-down to finish.*	**INTERVAL TRAINING** **34 mins (total)** *10 mins warm-up, then 7 x intervals of 60 secs brisk run/60 secs walk. 10 mins cool-down to finish.*
THURSDAY	REST	REST
FRIDAY	**TEMPO RUN** Learn how it feels to run at different paces. **30 mins (total)** *10 mins easy pace, followed by 10 mins faster pace, then 10 mins easy pace to finish.* **Resistance B2**	**TEMPO RUN** **30 mins (total)** *10 mins easy pace, followed by 10 mins faster pace, then 10 mins easy pace to finish.* **Resistance B2**
SATURDAY	REST	REST
SUNDAY	**LONG SLOW DISTANCE RUN** Starting to build distance covered in one run or walk. Go at an easy pace at which you can chat. **70 mins** *Constant easy pace*	**LONG SLOW DISTANCE RUN/WALK** **85 mins** *Constant easy pace*

REST

STEADY RUN/WALK

40 mins   *Constant pace*

Resistance B1

INTERVAL TRAINING
The "brisk" intervals here should feel hard and you should not be able to talk while doing them. Slow right down for the jog to get your breath back.

36 mins (total)

10 mins warm-up, then 8 x intervals of 60 secs at a brisk run/60 secs at an easy jog. 10 mins cool-down to finish.

REST

TEMPO RUN

30 mins (total)

10 mins easy pace, followed by 10 mins faster pace, then 10 mins easy pace to finish.

Resistance B2

REST

LONG SLOW DISTANCE RUN

100 mins   *Constant easy pace*

TOP TIP # 8
MAKE RACE DAY MANAGEABLE

"I was dreading race day, but I found a few great ways of getting through it. Having my friends and family there and the support of the crowd was hugely motivating. I also broke the race down – I knew that each 45 minutes I could have a gel and I ticked off each of the mile markers to help make it seem more manageable. Imagining the feeling of crossing the finish line also helped spur me on through those final miles."

VICKY ELLISON

TOP TIP # 9
REWARD YOURSELF

"When you're training and racing hard, you need to reward yourself with the odd treat. I couldn't have done without my massage after the London Marathon – when Claire the lovely osteopath worked her magic and made me feel human again. The only problem was that I could have happily stayed there for the rest of the day!"

NELL MCANDREW

	4	**5**
MONDAY	REST	REST
TUESDAY	**STEADY RUN/WALK** **35 mins** *Constant pace* **Resistance B1**	**STEADY RUN/WALK** **40 mins** *Constant pace* **Resistance B1**
WEDNESDAY	**INTERVAL TRAINING** **30 mins (total)** *10 mins warm-up, then 5 x intervals of 60 secs at a brisk run/60 secs walk. 10 mins cool-down to finish.*	**INTERVAL TRAINING** **36 mins (total)** *10 mins warm-up, then 8 x intervals of 60 secs at a brisk run/60 secs jog. 10 mins cool-down to finish.*
THURSDAY	REST	REST
FRIDAY	**TEMPO RUN** **30 mins (total)** *10 mins easy pace, followed by 10 mins faster pace, then 10 mins easy pace to finish.* **Resistance B2**	**TEMPO RUN** **35 mins (total)** *10 mins easy pace, followed by 15 mins faster pace, then 10 mins easy pace to finish.* **Resistance B2**
SATURDAY	REST	REST
SUNDAY	**LONG SLOW DISTANCE RUN** **90 mins** *Constant easy pace*	**LONG SLOW DISTANCE RUN** **100 mins** *Constant easy pace*

REST

STEADY RUN

50 mins *Constant pace*

INTERVAL TRAINING

35 mins (total)

10 mins warm-up, then 6 x intervals of 90 secs at a brisk run/60 secs jog. 10 mins cool-down to finish.

Resistance B1

REST

TEMPO RUN

35 mins (total)

5 mins easy pace/10 mins faster/5 mins easy/10 mins faster/5 mins easy to finish.

Resistance B2

REST

LONG SLOW DISTANCE RUN

115 mins *Constant easy pace*

NAME: **VICKY**

AGE: **30**

PROFESSION: **MARKETING MANAGER**

EVENT: **LONDON MARATHON**

WHAT WAS YOUR GOAL BEFORE YOUR RUN?
I entered my first 10K race having only ever run one event – a 5K – a few years before. At the 5K I struggled a lot and had to stop and walk several times. For the 10K, my goal was just to keep running for the whole distance without stopping. I managed this and decided to set myself the same goal but over a much longer distance – the marathon.

HOW LONG WAS YOUR TRAINING PLAN?
I followed Matt's 16-week plan.

DID YOU COMPLETE ALL OF THE PLAN?
Mostly. I missed a run here and there because of other commitments, but I stuck to the plan as much as possible. If I had to miss a session, I tried to shuffle my diary around to make up for it.

HOW DID YOU FIND THE TRAINING?
Getting out of the house was the hardest thing! I would take ages to get ready and always managed to find a million things I could do to delay starting, but once I did start I usually enjoyed the training. There were a few very rainy runs and some very cold ones too when I wondered why I was doing it, but I got an even greater sense of achievement from getting through those sessions.

	7	**8**
MONDAY	**Resistance B1**	REST
TUESDAY	**STEADY RUN** **60 mins** *Constant pace*	**STEADY RUN** **50 mins** *Constant pace*
WEDNESDAY	**INTERVAL TRAINING** **40 mins (total)** *10 mins warm-up, then 8 x intervals of 90 secs at a brisk run/60 secs jog. 10 mins cool-down to finish.* **Resistance B2**	**INTERVAL TRAINING** We're now throwing in a few 30-second sprints for some serious speed and fun. Stride out and keep your shoulders relaxed. **25 mins (total)** *10 mins warm-up, then 5 x 30 secs sprint/30 secs jog. 5 mins cool-down to finish.* **Resistance B2**
THURSDAY	REST	REST
FRIDAY	**TEMPO RUN** **39 mins (total)** *5 mins easy pace/12 mins faster/5 mins easy/12 mins faster/5 mins easy to finish.* **Resistance B1**	**TEMPO RUN** **35 mins (total)** *5 mins easy pace/10 mins faster/5 mins easy/10 mins faster/5 mins easy to finish.* **Resistance B1**
SATURDAY	REST	REST
SUNDAY	**LONG SLOW DISTANCE RUN** **125 mins** *Constant easy pace*	**LONG SLOW DISTANCE RUN** **120 mins** *Constant easy pace*

Resistance B1

STEADY RUN

55 mins *Constant pace*

INTERVAL TRAINING

40 mins (total)

10 mins warm-up, then 8 x intervals of 90 secs at a brisk run/60 secs jog. 10 mins cool-down to finish.

Resistance B2

REST

TEMPO RUN

39 mins (total)

5 mins easy pace/12 mins faster/5 mins easy/12 mins faster/5 mins easy to finish.

Resistance B1

REST

LONG SLOW DISTANCE RUN
In place of this long distance run, why not enter a half marathon race?

135 mins *Constant easy pace*

HOW DID YOU COPE WITH SETBACKS, SUCH AS SMALL INJURIES OR ILLNESS?

I was very lucky not to have too much injury trouble. Muscle tightness was the main problem I experienced but I made sure I used a foam roller every day (even when I wasn't running) and I had a couple of sports massages, which really helped. I got a cold a few weeks before the marathon which stayed with me for over a week and made me feel exhausted but I took extra vitamin C, made sure I ate well and got lots of sleep and eventually felt better.

WAS THERE SOMETHING THAT YOU DISCOVERED THAT HELPED YOU TRAIN?

A great pair of trainers was invaluable. I used to get squashed second toes but someone recommended toe covers to me and they really helped. Energy gels were also great for longer runs and taking rehydration tablets afterwards helped too. My GPS running watch was good too – knowing your pace is so useful and tracking your progress is great for motivation.

WHAT WAS THE ONE THING THAT YOU COULD NOT HAVE DONE IT WITHOUT?

The support of my friends and family.

HOW DID YOU KEEP YOURSELF MOTIVATED?

Raising money for a charity really helped keep me going, knowing that friends and family had been so generous in their support. It also helped me to follow a plan and tick off each training session day by day. Looking at the whole plan was more daunting, so breaking it down helped a lot. Changing my route and my Ipod playlist motivated me and having little goals like running to a certain landmark also helped. Entering smaller races in the lead-up to the marathon gave me confidence for the real event as they gave me a sense of achievement as I completed longer and longer distances.

WHAT WOULD YOU CHANGE ABOUT YOUR PREPARATION NEXT TIME?

I would try to persuade more friends to enter. Running alone is great but sometimes it's nice to run with a friend.

	10	11
MONDAY	Resistance B2	Resistance B1
TUESDAY	**STEADY RUN** **65 mins** *Constant pace*	**STEADY RUN** **75 mins** *Constant pace*
WEDNESDAY	**HILL TRAINING** To build leg strength, introduce some hills into your interval training. Push on the uphill and make the downhill an easy jog. **32 mins (total)** *10 mins warm-up, then on a 200m hill, run 6 hills. Jog back down to recover between each. Cool down for 10 mins to finish.*	**INTERVAL TRAINING** **44 mins (total)** *10 mins warm-up, then 8 x intervals of 2 mins brisk run/ 1 min jog. 10 mins cool-down to finish.*
THURSDAY	REST	REST
FRIDAY	**TEMPO RUN** **45 mins (total)** *5 mins easy pace/15 mins faster/5 mins easy/15 mins faster/5 mins easy to finish.* **Resistance B2**	**PACING RUN** Pick an out and back route. Run a steady pace for the outbound leg and try to keep the same pace for the return leg. **45 mins (total)** *20 mins out at a steady pace followed by 20 mins back to start at the same pace. 5 mins easy cool-down to finish.* **Resistance B2**
SATURDAY	REST	REST
SUNDAY	**LONG SLOW DISTANCE RUN** **150 mins** *Constant easy pace*	**LONG SLOW DISTANCE RUN** **165 mins** *Constant easy pace*

Resistance B1

STEADY RUN

60 mins   *Constant pace*

INTERVAL TRAINING

30 mins (total)

10 mins warm-up, then 10 x intervals of 30 secs sprint/30 secs jog. 10 mins cool-down to finish.

Resistance B2

STEADY RUN

30 mins   *Constant pace*

REST

PRACTICE RACE

Find a long road race to enter for today's session. Anything with a distance of 15–21 miles would be ideal.

120–160 mins   *Race pace*

TOP TIP # 10
IT'S NEVER TOO LATE TO START!

"If I could offer one piece of advice about running over all others it's that it's never too late to put on those running shoes for the first time. My mum was 54 and had never done any running at all when I encouraged her to walk a 5K Race for Life. She started by following my suggestion that she jog for 1 minute, then walk for 1 minute before gradually building up the time she spent jogging. Soon she was running the same distance, and not long afterwards she was taking part in 10K runs, the Great North Run (a half marathon) and, finally, completing the London Marathon. I am *so* proud of her and always mention her when people say that they can't run. Once you complete your first run, whatever the distance, you feel such a huge sense of achievement. Before you know it, you're addicted!"

NELL MCANDREW

	13	**14**
MONDAY	Resistance B1	Resistance B1
TUESDAY	**STEADY RUN** **70 mins** _Constant pace_	**STEADY RUN** **60 mins** _Constant pace_
WEDNESDAY	**INTERVAL TRAINING** The fast intervals here should be at your 10K pace or about 80% effort. Slow right down for the jog to get your breath back. **44 mins (total)** _10 mins warm-up, then 6 x intervals of 3 mins fast run/60 secs jog. 10 mins cool-down to finish._	**HILL TRAINING** **36 mins (total)** _10 mins warm-up, then on a 200m hill, run 8 hills. Jog back down to recover between each. Cool-down for 10 mins to finish._
THURSDAY	Resistance B2	REST
FRIDAY	**TEMPO RUN** **51 mins (total)** _5 mins easy pace/18 mins faster/5 mins easy/18 mins faster/5 mins easy to finish._	**TEMPO RUN** **55 mins (total)** _5 mins easy pace/20 mins faster/5 mins easy/20 mins faster/5 mins easy to finish._
SATURDAY	REST	REST
SUNDAY	**LONG SLOW DISTANCE RUN** **180 mins** _Constant easy pace_	**LONG SLOW DISTANCE RUN** **120 mins** _Constant easy pace_

REST

REST

STEADY RUN
Run at a relaxed pace

50 mins   *Constant pace*

STEADY RUN
Get out for a run, it should feel easy and enjoyable.

30 mins   *Constant pace*

INTERVAL TRAINING

40 mins (total)

10 mins warm-up, then 10 x intervals of 90 secs fast run/30 secs jog. 10 mins cool-down to finish.

INTERVAL TRAINING
A few final sprint blasts to blow those cobwebs away.

25 mins (total)

10 mins warm-up, then 5 x intervals of 30 secs sprint/30 secs jog. 10 mins cool-down to finish.

REST

REST

TEMPO RUN

45 mins (total)

5 mins easy pace/15 mins faster/5 mins easy/15 mins faster/5 mins easy to finish.

EASY RUN
Stretch your legs out and take it easy before the big day. This may feel hard, but it's just nerves. You are ready to race.

20 mins   *Constant pace*

REST

REST

LONG SLOW DISTANCE RUN
The distance covered is tapering down before your race. This should feel easy and really comfortable.

75 mins   *Easy pace, but consistent*

RACE DAY

You've made it, only 26.2 miles to go. Enjoy it, you've worked hard!

	1	**2**
MONDAY	REST	REST
	PB As above.	PB As above.
TUESDAY	**INTERVAL TRAINING** **35 mins (total)** *10 mins warm-up, then 5 x intervals of 2 mins at 85% MHR/60 secs slow jog or walk. 10 mins cool-down to finish.* PB Fartlek A session (track).	**INTERVAL TRAINING** **38 mins (total)** *10 mins warm up, then 6 x 2 mins at 85% MHR/60 secs slow jog or walk. 10 mins cool-down to finish.* **Resistance A1** PB 5 mins warm-up, then 7 x intervals of 90 secs 85% MHR/60 secs slow jog or walk. 5 mins cool-down to finish.
WEDNESDAY	**STEADY RUN** Getting time on your feet. Run at a pace at which you can still chat. **45 mins** *Constant pace (70% MHR)* **Resistance A1** PB Steady run as above; Resistance A1.	**STEADY RUN** **45 mins** *Constant pace (70% MHR)* PB Steady run as above; Resistance A1.
THURSDAY	**TEMPO RUN** **40 mins (total)** *10 mins easy pace, followed by 20 mins faster pace at 80% MHR, then 10 mins easy cool-down to finish.* PB As above.	**TEMPO RUN** **40 mins (total)** *10 mins easy pace, followed by 20 mins faster pace at 80% MHR, then 10 mins easy cool-down to finish.* **Resistance A2** PB As above.
FRIDAY	REST	REST
	PB As above.	PB As above.
SATURDAY	**THRESHOLD RUN** Run this track-based session at a speed that is equivalent to 3–5K race pace. **20–30 mins (track)** **Resistance A2** PB Threshold run as above.	**STEADY RUN** **45 mins** *Constant pace (70% MHR)* **Resistance A2** PB Steady run as above; Resistance A2.
SUNDAY	**LONG SLOW DISTANCE RUN** **70 mins** *Constant easy pace (60% MHR)* PB As above.	**LONG SLOW DISTANCE RUN** **85 mins** *Constant easy pace (60% MHR)* PB As above.

REST

PB As above.

INTERVAL TRAINING
44 mins (total)

10 mins warm-up, then 6 x 3 mins at 85% MHR/60 secs slow jog or walk. 10 mins cool-down to finish.

Resistance A2

PB Maximum intensity intervals session A (track).

STEADY RUN

50 mins Constant pace (70% MHR)

PB As above.

TEMPO RUN
39 mins (total)

2 x 5 mins easy pace/12 mins faster at 80% MHR. 5 mins easy pace to finish.

Resistance A1

PB Tempo run of 10 mins easy pace/20 mins 80% MHR/10 mins easy cool-down to finish.

REST

PB Resistance A2.

STEADY RUN

50 mins *Constant pace (70% MHR)*
Resistance A2

PB As above.

LONG SLOW DISTANCE RUN

100 mins *Constant easy pace (60% MHR)*

PB As above.

FAST MARATHON

NAME: JENNI FALCONER

AGE: 35

PROFESSION: TELEVISION PRESENTER

EVENT: LONDON MARATHON

WHAT WAS YOUR GOAL BEFORE YOUR RUN?
For years I enjoyed running for pleasure with no challenges or real goals. However, in 2009 I decided to set myself a challenge – to run a marathon. It was something I'd always secretly longed to do but feared disappointing myself by not achieving a respectable time. Training was difficult as with my work there was no set routine in my daily life to plan runs and training. When marathon day itself finally came I was incredibly nervous, but somehow I managed to get round! It was a hot day, but after 3 hours 53 minutes I reached the finish. As I crossed the line, I vowed never to do it again – I was hyperventilating, felt stiff and was truly exhausted. However, a few hours later, I'd already changed my mind! I soon agreed to run again in 2010, this time vowing to train properly. I met Matt and he introduced me to Karen at his gym who gave me a comprehensive programme with the aim to get my time down...ideally to 3.30.

HOW LONG WAS YOUR TRAINING PLAN?
16 weeks of training starting in January.

DID YOU COMPLETE ALL OF THE PLAN?
I completed as much of the plan as I could. My work was based out of London, which made the training process easier. I was completing 5 runs a week, one of which was a long run.

	4	**5**
MONDAY	**REST**	**REST**
	PB As above.	PB As above.
TUESDAY	**INTERVAL TRAINING** **28 mins (total)** *5 mins warm-up, then 6 x 2 mins at 85% MHR/60 secs slow jog or walk. 5 mins cool-down to finish.* **Resistance A1** PB Maximum intensity intervals session A (track).	**INTERVAL TRAINING** **45 mins (total)** *10 mins warm-up, then 5 x intervals of 4 mins at 85% MHR/60 secs slow jog or walk. 10 mins cool-down to finish.* PB 10 mins warm-up, then 6 x intervals of 4 mins 85% MHR/60 secs slow jog or walk. 10 mins cool-down to finish.
WEDNESDAY	**STEADY RUN** **40 mins** *Constant pace (70% MHR)* PB Steady run as above; Resistance A1.	**STEADY RUN** **50 mins** *Constant pace (70% MHR)* **Resistance A1** PB As above.
THURSDAY	**TEMPO RUN** **30 mins (total)** *5 mins easy pace, followed by 20 mins faster pace at 80% MHR, then 5 mins easy cool-down to finish.* **Resistance A2** PB Tempo run of 10 mins easy pace/25 mins 80% MHR/10 mins easy cool-down to finish.	**TEMPO RUN** **39 mins (total)** *5 mins easy pace/12 mins faster at 80% MHR/5 mins easy/12 mins faster at 80% MHR/5 mins easy pace to finish.* PB Tempo run of 10 mins easy pace/20 mins 80% MHR/10 mins easy cool-down to finish.
FRIDAY	**REST**	**REST**
	PB As above.	PB As above.
SATURDAY	**STEADY RUN** **45 mins** *Constant pace (70% MHR)* PB Steady run as above, Resistance A2.	**THRESHOLD RUN** **20–30 mins (track)** **Resistance A2** PB Threshold run session as above; Resistance A2.
SUNDAY	**LONG SLOW DISTANCE RUN** **90 mins** *Constant easy pace (60% MHR)* PB As above.	**LONG SLOW DISTANCE RUN** **100 mins** *Constant easy pace (60% MHR)* PB As above.

REST

PB As above.

HILL TRAINING
35 mins (total)

10 mins warm up then, on a 250m hill, run 6 hills. Jog back for 60 secs between each. 10 mins cool-down.

Resistance A1

PB 10 mins warm-up then, on a 200m hill, run 8 hills at 85% MHR. Jog back to recover between each. 10 mins cool-down to finish.

STEADY RUN

55 mins   *Constant pace (70% MHR)*

PB Steady run as above; Resistance A1.

TEMPO RUN
45 mins (total)

2 x 5 mins easy pace/15 mins faster at 80% MHR. 5 mins easy pace to finish.

Resistance A2

PB Maximum intensity intervals A (track).

REST

PB As above.

STEADY RUN

50 mins   *Constant pace (70% MHR)*
Resistance A1

PB 55-min run (constant pace) at 70% MHR.

LONG SLOW DISTANCE RUN

115 mins   *Constant easy pace (60% MHR)*

PB As above.

HOW DID YOU FIND THE TRAINING?
Although there were days when I couldn't be bothered, these were few and far between and tended to be because of really bad weather. On these days I would often choose to run on the treadmill instead of heading outdoors. Although I think of myself as a bit of a fair weather runner, while I was completing the training I found myself out running in wind, rain, snow, sun – all seasons. I truly found it addictive and loved it (most of the time!).

HOW DID YOU COPE WITH SETBACKS, SUCH AS SMALL INJURIES OR ILLNESS?
Injury-wise, I felt stiff from time to time, so started having fortnightly sports massages, which really helped. During the first few months of training I got a cold and did take a week off, but even during this period I kept up the weight sessions. When I came back, I felt rejuvenated and found that I was running stronger!

WAS THERE SOMETHING THAT YOU DISCOVERED THAT HELPED YOU TRAIN?
Running with a friend on the long run days helped enormously. We ran faster and further than we realised because we were chatting the whole way. I also found that energy gels helped give me the extra kick I needed on longer runs.

WHAT WAS THE ONE THING THAT YOU COULD NOT HAVE DONE WITHOUT?
I couldn't pick just one, but if I was allowed three I would say: good trainers, baths, and my iPod!

HOW DID YOU KEEP MOTIVATED?
Because of my competitive nature, I didn't really find that I had any problems keeping myself motivated. The fact that I was running for a great charity in CLIC Sargeant did help when I needed that little extra push.

WHAT WOULD YOU CHANGE ABOUT YOUR PREPARATION NEXT TIME?
You can always train harder and focus more. Next time I run I'll be a new mum – I have no idea how this will affect my training opportunities, but giving yourself plenty of time to prepare whatever your situation is key.

	7	8
MONDAY	**Resistance A2** PB As above.	REST PB As above.
TUESDAY	**INTERVAL TRAINING** **43 mins (total)** *5 mins warm-up, then 5 x (5 mins at 85% MHR/90 secs slow jog or walk). 5 mins cool-down to finish.* PB 5 mins warm-up, then 6 x intervals of 5 mins 85% MHR/90 secs slow jog or walk. 5 mins cool-down to finish.	**INTERVAL TRAINING** **28 mins (total)** *10 mins warm-up, then 8 x 30 secs sprint at 90% MHR/30 secs jog. 10 mins cool-down to finish.* **Resistance A1** PB Maximum intensity intervals session B (track).
WEDNESDAY	**STEADY RUN** **60 mins** *Constant pace (70% MHR)* PB As above.	**STEADY RUN** **50 mins** *Constant pace (70% MHR)* PB Steady run as above; Resistance A1.
THURSDAY	**PACING RUN** **45 mins (total)** *20 mins out at a steady pace (70% MHR) followed by 20 mins back to start at the same pace. 5 mins cool-down.* **Resistance A1** PB Tempo run as above.	**TEMPO RUN** **39 mins (total)** *2 x 5 mins easy pace/12 mins faster at 80% MHR. 5 mins easy pace to finish.* **Resistance A2** PB Tempo run of 10 mins easy pace/30 mins 80% MHR/10 mins easy cool down to finish.
FRIDAY	REST PB As above.	REST PB As above.
SATURDAY	**STEADY RUN** **55 mins** *Constant pace (70% MHR)* PB 60-min run (constant pace) at 70% MHR.	**STEADY RUN** **45 mins** *Constant pace (70% MHR)* **Resistance A1** PB 65-min run (constant pace) at 70% MHR; Resistance A2.
SUNDAY	**LONG SLOW DISTANCE RUN** **125 mins** *Constant easy pace (60% MHR)* PB As above.	**LONG SLOW DISTANCE RUN** **120 mins** *Constant easy pace (60% MHR)* PB As above.

REST

PB As above.

HILL TRAINING
38 mins (total)

10 mins warm-up then, on a 300m hill, run 6 hills. Jog back down between each. 10 mins cool-down to finish.

Resistance A2

PB 10 mins warm-up then, on a 300m hill, run 6 hills at 85% MHR. Jog back to recover between each. 10 mins cool-down to finish.

STEADY RUN

60 mins *Constant pace (70% MHR)*

PB Steady run as above; Resistance A1.

TEMPO RUN

51 mins (total)

5 mins easy pace/18 mins faster at 80% MHR/5 mins easy/18 mins faster at 80% MHR/5 mins easy pace to finish.

PB Tempo run of 3 x 5 mins easy pace/15 mins 80% MHR.

REST

PB As above.

THRESHOLD RUN
Skip this session if racing tomorrow.

20–30 mins (track)

Resistance A1

PB 40-min threshold run session (track); Resistance A2.

LONG SLOW DISTANCE RUN
Or HALF MARATHON
If you've entered a half marathon today, enjoy it! Otherwise, complete the run stated below.
135 mins *Constant easy pace (60% MHR)*

PB As above.

FAST MARATHON

NAME: **NELL MCANDREW**

AGE: **38**

PROFESSION: **MODEL & PRESENTER**

EVENT: **LONDON MARATHON**

WHAT WAS YOUR GOAL BEFORE YOUR RUN?
I enjoy running and have completed quite a few races in the past. As Cancer Research UK's running ambassador, I really have to walk the walk (or run the run, I suppose!), completing a number of runs of varying distances. I have run the London Marathon five times previously and this year I recorded my personal best of 3 hours 8 minutes – so I am improving with age!

HOW LONG WAS YOUR TRAINING PLAN?
I keep fit all year round and have always just tried to fit my running in as and when I can. When I know the marathon is coming up, I do try and be more consistent and do 12 weeks of specific training. I would definitely recommend longer than this for anyone who isn't used to running, though.

DID YOU COMPLETE ALL OF THE PLAN?
To be honest, I've never really followed a strict plan – I just try to do as much as I can to know I can complete the race distance. I always feel that if I could be more strict with my training plan and diet I would definitely be able to run faster, but as a mother I do find it hard to stick to a fixed running regime and find myself having to juggle my running around cooking, cleaning, the school run, housework, bath time, etc.! Running is my passion but being a mum is my priority.

	10	11
MONDAY	REST	REST
	PB As above.	PB As above.
TUESDAY	**INTERVAL PYRAMID RUN** **41 mins (total)** *5 mins warm-up, then 3/5/7/5/3 mins at 85% MHR with 90 secs recovery between each run. 5 mins easy* **Resistance A2** PB 5 mins warm up, then pyramid intervals of 4/6/8/6/4 mins at 85% MHR with 90 secs jog between each run. 5 mins cool-down to finish.	**KENYAN HILLS** **43 mins (total)** *10 mins warm-up, then 4 x run uphill and downhill for 5 mins/2 mins recovery jog. 5 mins cool-down to finish.* PB Threshold runs session (track).
WEDNESDAY	**STEADY RUN** **65 mins** *Constant pace (70% MHR)* PB Steady run as above; Resistance A1.	**STEADY RUN** **70 mins** *Constant pace (70% MHR)* PB Steady run as above; Resistance A1.
THURSDAY	**TEMPO RUN** **55 mins (total)** *5 mins easy pace/20 mins faster at 80% MHR/5 mins easy/20 mins faster at 80% MHR/5 mins easy pace to finish.* PB Tempo run of 10 mins easy pace/40 mins 80% MHR/10 mins easy cool-down to finish.	**PACING RUN** **55 mins (total)** *25 mins out at a steady pace (70% MHR) followed by 25 mins back to start at the same pace. 5 mins easy cool down to finish.* PB Tempo run of 3 x 5mins easy pace/15 mins 80% MHR. 5 mins cool-down to finish.
FRIDAY	REST	**Resistance A1**
	PB As above.	PB REST
SATURDAY	**STEADY RUN** **65 mins** *Constant pace (70% MHR)* **Resistance A1** PB Steady run as above; Resistance A2.	**STEADY RUN** **70 mins** *Constant pace (70% MHR)* PB Steady run as above; Resistance A2.
SUNDAY	**LONG SLOW DISTANCE RUN** **150 mins** *Easy pace (60% MHR) for 135 mins, then last 15 mins at your target marathon pace.* PB As above.	**LONG SLOW DISTANCE RUN** **165 mins** *Easy pace (60% MHR) for 145 mins, then last 20 mins at your target marathon pace.* PB As above.

REST

PB As above.

INTERVAL TRAINING
30 mins (total)

10 mins warm-up, then 10 x 30 secs sprint/30 secs jog. 10 mins cool-down to finish.

Resistance A2

PB 10 mins warm-up, then 15 x intervals of 30 secs sprint at 90% MHR/30 secs slow jog. 10 mins cool-down to finish.

STEADY RUN

60 mins   *Constant pace (70% MHR)*

PB Steady run as above; Resistance A1.

STEADY RUN

30 mins   *Constant pace*

Resistance A1

PB 45-min run (constant pace) at 75% MHR.

REST

PB As above.

STEADY RUN

30 mins   *Constant pace (70% MHR)*

PB 45-min run (constant pace) at 70% MHR; Resistance A2.

PRACTICE RACE

120–160 mins   *Race pace*

PB As above.

WAS THERE SOMETHING THAT YOU DISCOVERED THAT HELPED YOU TRAIN?
It's very important to be comfortable when running, so getting your clothing and footwear correct is a must. Wearing the right type of trainer for my running style has been a great help in making sure I am comfortable. I also always wear proper running socks as I feel this helps to prevent blisters. Getting my nutrition right is also important to make certain that I am running at my best. I always eat a proper breakfast before exercising: porridge, a banana and sometimes toast if I'm about to head off on a long run. I am a chocoholic and love cakes but always feel that I have earned them as I exercise so much!

WHAT WAS THE ONE THING THAT YOU COULDN'T HAVE DONE WITHOUT?
Doing my long run once a week. It wasn't always something I looked forward to but I believe it really helped me to get used to running for a long period of time. My longest run while training was a steady 24 miles. It seemed to go on forever, but once I had done it I had peace of mind that I could do the marathon.

HOW DID YOU KEEP MOTIVATED?
I really struggled at the beginning of the year as I had a terrible flu virus twice, so constantly felt run down. As most parents who have young children do, I seem to get every bug going. During this time I focused on how fortunate I was to be offered a place for the London Marathon as I know many people who apply and are not successful. I also had the added incentive of not wanting to let my charity down. I really recommend signing up to run for a charity as it helps keep you motivated as you know your efforts are helping support a worthy cause.

WHAT WOULD YOU CHANGE ABOUT YOUR PREPARATION NEXT TIME?
I would train harder! I would also add one speed session a week to my training as I think this would help me increase my pace and enable me to run faster.

	13	**14**
MONDAY	REST	REST
	PB As above.	PB As above.
TUESDAY	**SPRINT FINISH TRAINING** **50 mins (total)** *5 mins warm-up, then 8 x (3 ½ mins at 80% MHR/30 secs at 95% MHR/1 min recovery). 5 mins cool-down to finish.* **Resistance A1** PB Maximum intensity intervals session A (track).	**KENYAN HILLS** **50 mins (total)** *10 mins warm-up, then 5 x run uphill and downhill for 5 mins/2 mins recovery jog. 5 mins cool-down to finish.* PB Fartlek training B session (track).
WEDNESDAY	**STEADY RUN** **75 mins** *Constant pace (70% MHR)* PB As above.	**STEADY RUN** **65 mins** *Constant pace (70% MHR)* PB As above.
THURSDAY	**TEMPO RUN** **65 mins (total)** *3 x 5 mins easy pace/15 mins faster at 80% MHR. 5 mins easy pace to finish.* **Resistance A2** PB As above.	**PACING RUN** **65 mins (total)** *30 mins out at a steady pace (70% MHR) followed by 30 mins back to start at the same pace. 5 mins easy cool-down to finish.* PB As above.
FRIDAY	REST	REST
	PB As above.	PB As above.
SATURDAY	**STEADY RUN** **60 mins** *Constant pace (70% MHR)* PB 70-min run (constant pace) at 70% MHR.	**THRESHOLD RUN** **20–30 mins** **Resistance A1** PB 45-min threshold run session (track).
SUNDAY	**LONG SLOW DISTANCE RUN** **180 mins** *Easy pace (60% MHR) for 150 mins, then last 30 mins at your target marathon pace.* PB As above.	**LONG SLOW DISTANCE RUN** **120 mins** *Easy pace (60% MHR) for 80 mins, then last 40 mins at your target marathon pace.* PB As above.

Resistance A2	**REST**
PB As above.	PB As above.

INTERVAL TRAINING

40 mins (total)

10 mins warm up, then 10 x 90 fast run/30 secs jog. 10 mins cool down to finish.

PB 10 mins warm-up, then 14 x intervals of 60 secs run at 85% MHR/30 secs jog. 10 mins cool-down to finish.

INTERVAL TRAINING

25 mins (total)

10 mins warm-up, then 5 x 30 secs sprint/30 secs jog. 10 mins cool-down to finish.

PB 10 mins warm-up, then 5 x intervals of 30 secs sprint at 90% MHR/30 secs jog. 10 mins cool-down to finish.

STEADY RUN

50 mins   *Constant pace (70% MHR)*

PB As above.

STEADY RUN

30 mins   *Constant pace (70% MHR)*

PB As above.

TEMPO RUN

45 mins (total)

5 mins easy pace/15 mins faster at 80% MHR/5 mins easy/15 mins faster at 80% MHR/5 mins easy pace to finish.

PB As above.

EASY RUN

20 mins   *Constant easy pace (60% MHR)*

PB As above.

REST

PB As above.

REST

PB As above.

STEADY RUN

60 mins   *Constant pace (70% MHR)*

PB 30-min run (constant pace) at 70% MHR.

VERY SHORT RUN

15 mins

PB As above.

LONG SLOW DISTANCE RUN

75 mins   *Constant easy pace (60% MHR)*

PB As above.

RACE DAY

You've made it, only 26.2 miles to go. Enjoy it, you've worked hard!

For an increasing number of people, running a marathon is not enough. Where once the first question asked of any serious runner was "have you run a marathon?" it seems now to be "how many have you run?". This has led many runners to a search for a new challenge and a higher goal, which is where ultra-distance events come in. These events mark out the running "super achievers". They give their participants running bragging rights and are the ultimate symbol of running success –the athletic equivalent of the sports car purchase or the trophy wife!

While ultra-distance events may not be for everybody, they certainly represent a potentially massive and rewarding challenge for a surprising number of people. Provided you are generally fit, healthy and experienced in running there is no reason why you shouldn't consider lining yourself up for an ultra-distance challenge. If you are new to running however, I would suggest that you don't even think about this section until you are at least a year down the line and have completed at least one marathon on the way – these events are brutal.

Although the specific training programme here is 32 weeks in duration, you should think of the process of preparation for this type of event as taking about a year. The first 20 weeks should be time in which you will be sorting out any physical issues you may have – any outstanding niggling injuries, problems with your running gait and technique or general fitness issues – before embarking on the intensive period of training outlined here. The training for the event takes serious mental and physical discipline and there is little room for movement or for lapses in the routine. Every day of training counts if you are going to succeed, so you need to plan your life to allow for such a disciplined existence.

With ultra-distance events varying from 30 miles through to 150 miles; some non-stop, some through mixed terrain, some in extreme heat and some in extreme cold, this is an event that can offer up whatever extreme challenge you feel you need to conquer. You may view it as being the defining moment of your running achievements, or simply as the gateway to a greater array of bigger, more challenging events. Whichever it is, remember to enjoy the process – feeling fulfilled, motivated and healthy in what you are doing – and you will be sure to surprise yourself with what you can achieve.

ULTRA
DISTANCE

	1	2
MONDAY	**STEADY RUN** Getting time on your feet. Run at a pace at which you can still chat. **1 hour** *Constant pace (60% MHR)*	**STEADY RUN** **40 mins** *Constant pace (60% MHR)*
TUESDAY	**INTERVAL TRAINING** Its early days, but we're laying the ground work for gaining some speed. Your recovery is a slow jog or walk. **5 x 800m intervals** *Intervals at 80% MHR with 200m jog between intervals.*	**INTERVAL TRAINING** **5 x 800m intervals** *Intervals at 80% MHR with 200m jog between intervals.*
WEDNESDAY	**TEMPO RUN** Leg strength is key for injury protection and efficient running style. Tempo running is faster than normal pace at 80% MHR. **20 mins (total)** *5 mins easy pace, followed by 10 mins faster pace at 80% MHR, then 5 mins easy pace to finish.* **Resistance A1**	**TEMPO RUN** **20 mins (total)** *5 mins easy pace, followed by 10 mins faster pace at 80% MHR, then 5 mins easy pace to finish.* **Resistance A2**
THURSDAY	REST	REST
FRIDAY	**HILL TRAINING** These hill intervals are designed to build leg strength and a high knee lift. **60 mins (total)** *5 mins warm-up, then on a 350m hill, run 15 hills at 80% MHR. Jog down for 1 min to recover between each. 10 mins cool-down to finish.*	**HILL TRAINING** **60 mins (total)** *5 mins warm-up, then on a 350m hill, run 15 hills at 80–90% MHR. Jog down for 1 min to recover between each. 10 mins cool-down to finish.*
SATURDAY	REST	REST
SUNDAY	**LONG SLOW DISTANCE RUN** Starting to build distance covered in one run. Run at an easy pace at which you can still chat. **2 hours** *Constant pace (60% MHR)*	**LONG SLOW DISTANCE RUN** **2 hours** *Constant pace (60% MHR)*

STEADY RUN

40 mins *Constant pace (60% MHR)*

STEADY RUN

40 mins *Constant pace (60% MHR)*

INTERVAL TRAINING

6 x 800m intervals

Intervals at 80% MHR with 200m jog between intervals.

INTERVAL TRAINING

6 x 800m intervals

Intervals at 80% MHR with 200m jog between intervals.

TEMPO RUN

20 mins (total)

5 mins easy pace, followed by 10 mins faster pace at 80% MHR, then 5 mins easy pace to finish.

Resistance A1

TEMPO RUN

20 mins (total)

5 mins easy pace, followed by 10 mins faster pace at 80% MHR, then 5 mins easy pace to finish.

Resistance A2

REST

REST

HILL TRAINING

70 mins (total)

5 mins warm-up, then on a 350m hill, run 20 hills at 80–90% MHR. Jog down to recover between each. 5 mins cool-down to finish.

HILL TRAINING

70 mins (total)

5 mins warm-up, then on a 350m hill, run 20 hills at 80–90% MHR. Jog down to recover between each. 5 mins cool-down to finish.

REST

REST

To protect your skin against burning in summer, don't forget to apply sun cream before your run.

LONG SLOW DISTANCE RUN

2 1/4 hours *Constant pace (60% MHR)*

LONG SLOW DISTANCE RUN

2 1/4 hours *Constant pace (60% MHR)*

	5	6
MONDAY	**STEADY RUN** **40 mins** *Constant pace (60% MHR)*	**STEADY RUN** **40 mins** *Constant pace (60% MHR)*
TUESDAY	**INTERVAL TRAINING** **6 x 800m intervals** *Intervals at 80% MHR with 200m jog between intervals.*	**INTERVAL TRAINING** **7 x 800m intervals** *Intervals at 80% MHR with 200m jog between intervals.*
WEDNESDAY	**TEMPO RUN** **20 mins (total)** *5 mins easy pace, followed by 10 mins faster pace at 80% MHR, then 5 mins easy pace to finish.* **Resistance A1**	**TEMPO RUN** **20 mins (total)** *5 mins easy pace, followed by 10 mins faster pace at 80% MHR, then 5 mins easy pace to finish.* **Resistance A2**
THURSDAY	REST	REST
FRIDAY	**HILL REPEATS** **70 mins (total)** *5 mins warm up, then on a 350m hill, run 20 hills at 80–90% MHR. Jog down to recover between each. 5 mins cool down to finish.*	**HILL REPEATS** **70 mins (total)** *5 mins warm up, then on a 350m hill, run 20 hills at 80–90% MHR. Jog down to recover between each. 5 mins cool down to finish.*
SATURDAY	REST	REST
SUNDAY	**LONG SLOW DISTANCE RUN** **1 ½ hours** *Constant pace (60% MHR)*	**LONG SLOW DISTANCE RUN** **2 ½ hours** *Constant pace (60% MHR)*

STEADY RUN
40 mins   *Constant pace (60% MHR)*

INTERVAL TRAINING
7 x 800m intervals
Intervals at 80% MHR with 200m jog between intervals.

TEMPO RUN
20 mins (total)
5 mins easy pace, followed by 10 mins faster pace at 80% MHR, then 5 mins easy pace to finish.
Resistance A1

HILL TRAINING
75 mins (total)
5 mins warm-up, then on a 350m hill, run 15 hills at 80–90% MHR. Jog down to recover between each. 10 mins cool-down to finish.

REST

LONG SLOW DISTANCE RUN
2 ½ hours   *Constant Pace (60% MHR)*

LONG SLOW DISTANCE RUN
1 hour   *Constant pace (60% MHR)*

ULTRA DISTANCE

NAME: **AYO WILLIAMS**

AGE: **34**

PROFESSION: **MANAGER**

EVENT: **MARATHON DES SABLES**

WHAT WAS YOUR GOAL BEFORE YOUR RUN?
To finish the race in the top half of the field, and to be fit and strong enough to genuinely enjoy it and soak up the atmosphere.

HOW LONG WAS YOUR TRAINING PROGRAMME?
My training programme was 6 months long, although I was probably decent half marathon fit at the start of the programme.

DID YOU COMPLETE ALL OF THE PLAN THAT YOU SHOULD HAVE?
I completed the training plan having only missed approximately six sessions due to injury, illness or over-indulgences from "special occasions".

DID YOU FIND THE TRAINING EASY, OR WERE THERE MOMENTS WHEN YOU FOUND THE GOING TOUGH?
The training was extremely tough. The long runs were savage, and without discipline and diligence they could easily have robbed me of my weekends! When I didn't get my food and drink intake consistent and appropriate, I did feel drained, and drinking alcohol became an issue as it made long runs the next day far harder! The rest days and easier weeks (every 4/5 weeks) were a welcome break in intensity, and felt great.

	8	**9**
MONDAY	**STEADY RUN** **40 mins** *Constant pace (60% MHR)*	**REST**
TUESDAY	**INTERVAL TRAINING** **7 x 800m intervals** *Intervals at 80% MHR with 200m jog between intervals.*	**INTERVAL TRAINING** **8 x 800m intervals** *Intervals at 80% MHR with 200m jog between intervals.*
WEDNESDAY	**TEMPO RUN** **20 mins (total)** *5 mins easy pace, followed by 10 mins faster pace at 80% MHR, then 5 mins easy pace to finish.* **Resistance A2**	**TEMPO RUN** **20 mins (total)** *5 mins easy pace, followed by 10 mins faster pace at 80% MHR, then 5 mins easy pace to finish.* **Resistance A1**
THURSDAY	**HILL TRAINING** **80 mins (total)** *10 mins warm-up, then on a 350m hill, run 15 hills at 80–90% MHR. Jog down to recover between each. 10 mins cool-down to finish.*	**HILL TRAINING** **85 mins (total)** *5 mins warm up, then on a 350m hill, run 15 hills at 80–90% MHR. Jog down to recover between each. 10 mins cool down to finish.*
FRIDAY	**REST**	**REST**
SATURDAY	**LONG SLOW DISTANCE** **2 ½ hours** *Constant Pace (60% MHR)*	**LONG SLOW DISTANCE RUN** **2 ½ hours** *Constant Pace (60% MHR)*
SUNDAY	**LONG SLOW DISTANCE RUN** **1 ½ hours** *Constant pace (60% MHR)*	**LONG SLOW DISTANCE RUN** **1 ¾ hours** *Constant pace (60% MHR)*

REST

INTERVAL TRAINING

8 x 800m intervals

Intervals at 80% MHR with 200m jog between intervals.

TEMPO RUN

20 mins (total)

5 mins easy pace, followed by 10 mins faster pace at 80% MHR, then 5 mins easy pace to finish.

Resistance A2

HILL TRAINING

85 mins (total)

5 mins warm up, then on a 350m hill, run 15 hills at 80–90% MHR. Jog down to recover between each. 10 mins cool down to finish.

REST

LONG SLOW DISTANCE RUN

2 ½ hours   *Constant Pace (60% MHR)*

LONG SLOW DISTANCE RUN

2 hours   *Constant pace (60% MHR)*

HOW DID YOU COPE WITH SETBACKS, SUCH AS SMALL INJURIES OR ILLNESS?

Setbacks were demoralising, but I coped mainly by telling myself that the odd session that I was forced to miss was ok, as long as I didn't miss any out of laziness. Illness was unavoidable, and I kept injuries to a minimum by observing rest days, foam rolling every day and very occasionally swapping in a spin bike or cross-trainer if my knees felt like they needed a break.

WAS THERE SOMETHING THAT YOU DISCOVERED THAT HELPED YOU TRAIN?

I found that filling up my MP3 player with things other than just music on the long runs helped a lot; I found some great comedy which helped break up the run well. Food-wise, salami sausage was a surprise find – it was easy to eat on the move and made a very welcome savoury change, from all the sweet gels, goos and energy drinks.

HOW DID YOU KEEP YOURSELF MOTIVATED?

I couldn't have done it without the support of all the people who helped me train, sponsored me or lent encouragement. This is what keeps you going when the going gets tough.

During training, raising the money for charity was a big motivator as I would continually explain to potential sponsors who and what I was running for. During the race I was motivated primarily by a desire to get over the finish line! That's all, really. To be honest there was so much camaraderie and adrenaline during the race, motivation while there wasn't an issue.

WHAT WOULD YOU CHANGE ABOUT YOUR PREPARATION NEXT TIME?

Next time I would trial all the foods that I ate while racing during training and stick to the ones I knew! It was a schoolboy error but I tried something new while I was out there, when offered, and the next thing I knew I was very glad I packed the Imodium...

	11	**12**
MONDAY	REST	REST
TUESDAY	**INTERVAL TRAINING** **8 x 800m intervals** *Intervals at 80% MHR with 200m jog between intervals.*	**INTERVAL TRAINING** **6 x 1000m intervals** *Intervals at 80% MHR with 200m jog between intervals.*
WEDNESDAY	**TEMPO RUN** **20 mins (total)** *5 mins easy pace, followed by 10 mins faster pace at 80% MHR, then 5 mins easy pace to finish.* **Resistance A1**	**TEMPO RUN** **20 mins (total)** *5 mins easy pace, followed by 10 mins faster pace at 80% MHR, then 5 mins easy pace to finish.* **Resistance A2**
THURSDAY	**HILL TRAINING** **90 mins (total)** *5 mins warm-up, then on a 350m hill, run 20 hills at 80–90% MHR. Jog down to recover between each. 5 mins cool-down to finish.*	**HILL TRAINING** **90 mins (total)** *5 mins warm-up, then on a 350m hill, run 20 hills at 80–90% MHR. Jog down to recover between each. 5 mins cool-down to finish.*
FRIDAY	REST	REST
SATURDAY	**LONG SLOW DISTANCE RUN** **3 ½ hours** *Constant Pace (60% MHR)*	**LONG SLOW DISTANCE RUN** **2 ½ hours** *Constant Pace (60% MHR)*
SUNDAY	**LONG SLOW DISTANCE RUN** **1 hour** *Constant pace (60% MHR)*	**LONG SLOW DISTANCE RUN** **2 ½ hours** *Constant pace (60% MHR)*

13	14
REST	**REST**

INTERVAL TRAINING

6 x 1,000m intervals

Intervals at 80% MHR with 200m jog between intervals.

INTERVAL TRAINING

6 x 1,000m intervals

Intervals at 80% MHR with 200m jog between intervals.

TEMPO RUN

20 mins (total)

5 mins easy pace, followed by 10 mins faster pace at 80% MHR, then 5 mins easy pace to finish.

Resistance A1

TEMPO RUN

20 mins (total)

5 mins easy pace, followed by 10 mins faster pace at 80% MHR, then 5 mins easy pace to finish.

Resistance A2

HILL TRAINING

90 mins (total)

5 mins warm-up, then on a 350m hill, run 20 hills at 80–90% MHR. Jog down to recover between each. 5 mins cool-down to finish.

HILL TRAINING

90 mins (total)

5 mins warm-up, then on a 350m hill, run 20 hills at 80–90% MHR. Jog down to recover between each. 5 mins cool-down to finish.

REST

REST

LONG SLOW DISTANCE RUN

2 ¾ hours   *Constant Pace (60% MHR)*

LONG SLOW DISTANCE RUN

3 hours   *Constant Pace (60% MHR)*

REST

REST

If you can, try to do your interval training on a track, where you can accurately judge the distances you are covering.

	15	16
MONDAY	REST	REST
TUESDAY	**INTERVAL TRAINING** **7 x 1,000m intervals** *Intervals at 80% MHR with 200m jog between intervals.*	**INTERVAL TRAINING** **7 x 1,000m intervals** *Intervals at 80% MHR with 200m jog between intervals.*
WEDNESDAY	**TEMPO RUN** **20 mins (total)** *5 mins easy pace, followed by 10 mins faster pace at 80% MHR, then 5 mins easy pace to finish.* **Resistance A1**	**TEMPO RUN** **20 mins (total)** *5 mins easy pace, followed by 10 mins faster pace at 80% MHR, then 5 mins easy pace to finish.* **Resistance A2**
THURSDAY	**HILL TRAINING** **90 mins (total)** *5 mins warm-up, then on a 350m hill, run 20 hills at 80–90% MHR. Jog down to recover between each. 5 mins cool-down to finish.*	**HILL TRAINING** **90 mins (total)** *5 mins warm-up, then on a 350m hill, run 20 hills at 80–90% MHR. Jog down to recover between each. 5 mins cool-down to finish.*
FRIDAY	REST	REST
SATURDAY	**LONG SLOW DISTANCE RUN** **3 hours** *Constant pace (60% MHR)*	**LONG SLOW DISTANCE RUN** **2 hours** *Constant Pace (60% MHR)*
SUNDAY	REST	**LONG SLOW DISTANCE RUN** **2 hours** *Constant pace (60% MHR)*

17

REST

INTERVAL TRAINING

7 x 1,000m intervals

Intervals at 80% MHR with 200m jog between intervals.

TEMPO RUN

20 mins (total)

5 mins easy pace, followed by 10 mins faster pace at 80% MHR, then 5 mins easy pace to finish.

Resistance A1

HILL TRAINING

90 mins (total)

5 mins warm-up, then on a 350m hill, run 20 hills at 80–90% MHR. Jog down to recover between each. 5 mins cool-down to finish.

REST

LONG SLOW DISTANCE RUN

3 ½ hours   *Constant Pace (60% MHR)*

LONG SLOW DISTANCE

2 ½ hours   *Constant pace (60% MHR)*

18

REST

INTERVAL TRAINING

8 x 1,000m intervals

Intervals at 80% MHR with 200m jog between intervals.

TEMPO RUN

20 mins (total)

5 mins easy pace, followed by 10 mins faster pace at 80% MHR, then 5 mins easy pace to finish.

Resistance A2

HILL TRAINING

90 mins (total)

5 mins warm-up, then on a 350m hill, run 20 hills at 80–90% MHR. Jog down to recover between each. 5 mins cool-down to finish.

REST

LONG SLOW DISTANCE RUN

3 ½ hours   *Constant Pace (60% MHR)*

LONG SLOW DISTANCE RUN

3 hours   *Constant pace (60% MHR)*

If you're finding the training sessions hard work, why not join a running club and run with others?

	19	**20**
MONDAY	REST	REST
TUESDAY	**INTERVAL TRAINING** **8 x 1,000m intervals** *Intervals at 80% MHR with 200m jog between intervals.*	**INTERVAL TRAINING** **8 x 1,000m intervals** *Intervals at 80% MHR with 200m jog between intervals.*
WEDNESDAY	**TEMPO RUN** **20 mins (total)** *5 mins easy pace, followed by 10 mins faster pace at 80% MHR, then 5 mins easy pace to finish.* **Resistance A1**	**TEMPO RUN** **20 mins (total)** *5 mins easy pace, followed by 10 mins faster pace at 80% MHR, then 5 mins easy pace to finish.* **Resistance A2**
THURSDAY	**HILL TRAINING** **90 mins (total)** *5 mins warm-up, then on a 350m hill, run 20 hills at 80–90% MHR. Jog down to recover between each. 5 mins cool-down to finish.*	**HILL TRAINING** **90 mins (total)** *5 mins warm-up, then on a 350m hill, run 20 hills at 80–90% MHR. Jog down to recover between each. 5 mins cool-down to finish.*
FRIDAY	REST	REST
SATURDAY	**LONG SLOW DISTANCE RUN** **2 ½ hours** — *Constant Pace (60% MHR)*	**LONG SLOW DISTANCE RUN** **4 hours** — *Constant Pace (60% MHR)*
SUNDAY	**LONG SLOW DISTANCE RUN** **2 ½ hours** — *Constant pace (60% MHR)*	**LONG SLOW DISTANCE RUN** **4 hours** — *Constant pace (60% MHR)*

REST

INTERVAL TRAINING
9 x 1,000m intervals

Intervals at 80% MHR with 200m jog between intervals.

TEMPO RUN
20 mins (total)

5 mins easy pace, followed by 10 mins faster pace at 80% MHR, then 5 mins easy pace to finish.

Resistance A1

HILL TRAINING
90 mins (total)

5 mins warm-up, then on a 350m hill, run 20 hills at 80–90% MHR. Jog down to recover between each. 5 mins cool-down to finish.

REST

LONG SLOW DISTANCE RUN
4 hours   *Constant Pace (60% MHR)*

LONG SLOW DISTANCE RUN
4 hours   *Constant pace (60% MHR)*

ULTRA DISTANCE

NAME: **TOM AITKENS**

AGE: **41**

PROFESSION: **CHEF**

EVENT: **MARATHON DES SABLES**

WHAT WAS YOUR GOAL BEFORE YOUR RUN?
I was training to run the 25th Marathon des Sables, which is 6 marathons back to back in the Sahara desert over 5 days. I had never run more than 3 miles before and I was 5 months away from the race, so I needed to get my skates on. Starting to run in October, I completed my first marathon by December the 21st.

HOW LONG WAS YOUR TRAINING PROGRAMME?
My training plan was 5 months long. During that time I had to get to a marathon distance first, before starting to run with a 12kg backpack by January to get practice in for carrying my bag while racing in the desert.

DID YOU COMPLETE ALL OF THE PLAN THAT YOU SHOULD HAVE?
Yes. I felt that I was well prepared – a result of the training that I was given by Jon at Matt's running clinic, which definitely gave me the strength and determination I needed to cover the distance.

DID YOU FIND THE TRAINING EASY?
The training is never easy! Although it was tough at times, you get through as it's the thought of what you are going to accomplish that makes you drive on.

	22	23
MONDAY	REST	REST
TUESDAY	**INTERVAL TRAINING** **9 x 1,000m intervals** *Intervals at 80% MHR with 200m jog between intervals.*	**INTERVAL TRAINING** **10 x 1,000m intervals** *Intervals at 80% MHR with 200m jog between intervals.*
WEDNESDAY	**TEMPO RUN** **20 mins (total)** *5 mins easy pace, followed by 10 mins faster pace at 80% MHR, then 5 mins easy pace to finish.* **Resistance A2**	**TEMPO RUN** **20 mins (total)** *5 mins easy pace, followed by 10 mins faster pace at 80% MHR, then 5 mins easy pace to finish.* **Resistance A1**
THURSDAY	**HILL TRAINING** **90 mins (total)** *5 mins warm-up, then on a 350m hill, run 20 hills at 80–90% MHR. Jog down to recover between each. 5 mins cool-down to finish.*	**HILL TRAINING** **90 mins (total)** *5 mins warm-up, then on a 350m hill, run 20 hills at 80–90% MHR. Jog down to recover between each. 5 mins cool-down to finish.*
FRIDAY	REST	REST
SATURDAY	**LONG SLOW DISTANCE RUN** **5 hours** *Constant Pace (60% MHR)*	**LONG SLOW DISTANCE RUN** **5 hours** *Constant Pace (60% MHR)*
SUNDAY	**LONG SLOW DISTANCE RUN** **5 hours** *Constant pace (60% MHR)*	**LONG SLOW DISTANCE RUN** **5 hours** *Constant pace (60% MHR)*

REST

INTERVAL TRAINING

10 x 1,000m intervals

Intervals at 80% MHR with 200m jog between intervals.

TEMPO RUN

20 mins (total)

5 mins easy pace, followed by 10 mins faster pace at 80% MHR, then 5 mins easy pace to finish.

Resistance A1

HILL TRAINING

90 mins (total)

5 mins warm-up, then on a 350m hill, run 20 hills at 80–90% MHR. Jog down to recover between each. 5 mins cool-down to finish.

REST

LONG SLOW DISTANCE RUN

5 hours   *Constant Pace (60% MHR)*

LONG SLOW DISTANCE RUN

5 hours   *Constant pace (60% MHR)*

HOW DID YOU COPE WITH SETBACKS, SUCH AS SMALL INJURIES OR ILLNESS?

I was very lucky that I did not get any injuries or setbacks at all during training. The only time I was ill was when I was out there as I got dehydrated due to the heat (temperatures can reach well over 40°C so this is not uncommon!).

WAS THERE SOMETHING THAT YOU DISCOVERED THAT HELPED YOU TRAIN OR COMPETE?

For me, the key was choosing the right kit to get through the race as well as making sure I consumed the correct combination of food, water and salt at the right times. In particular, I found the dehydrated expedition meals that are available to be a great way of getting the nutrition I needed for such an intense endurance effort.

HOW DID YOU KEEP YOURSELF MOTIVATED?

During training it was the thought of raising money for my chosen charity that spurred me on. During the race it was a question of never giving up and pushing on through that kept me going. Even when I was feeling awful – as my feet got totally trashed and infected as a result of running such a long distance in the desert conditions – I got through the pain by concentrating on the fact that there was someone else in the world who was suffering far worse than I was at that moment.

WHAT WOULD YOU CHANGE ABOUT YOUR PREPARATION NEXT TIME?

Nothing, really. I felt well prepared with the training I had.

	25	26
MONDAY	REST	REST
TUESDAY	**INTERVAL TRAINING** **10 x 1,000m intervals** *Intervals at 80% MHR with 200m jog between intervals.*	**INTERVAL TRAINING** **10 x 1,000m intervals** *Intervals at 80% MHR with 200m jog between intervals.*
WEDNESDAY	**TEMPO RUN** **20 mins (total)** *5 mins easy pace, followed by 10 mins faster pace at 80% MHR, then 5 mins easy pace to finish.* **Resistance A2**	REST
THURSDAY	**HILL TRAINING** **90 mins (total)** *5 mins warm-up, then on a 350m hill, run 20 hills at 80–90% MHR. Jog down to recover between each. 5 mins cool-down to finish.*	**HILL TRAINING** **90 mins (total)** *5 mins warm-up, then on a 350m hill, run 20 hills at 80–90% MHR. Jog down to recover between each. 5 mins cool-down to finish.*
FRIDAY	REST	REST
SATURDAY	**LONG SLOW DISTANCE RUN** **2 hours** *Constant pace (60% MHR)*	**LONG SLOW DISTANCE RUN** **5 hours** *Constant pace (60% MHR)*
SUNDAY	**LONG SLOW DISTANCE RUN** **2 hours** *Constant pace (60% MHR)*	**LONG SLOW DISTANCE RUN** **5 hours** *Constant pace (60% MHR)*

REST

INTERVAL TRAINING
10 x 1,000m intervals

Intervals at 80% MHR with 200m jog between intervals.

REST

HILL TRAINING
90 mins (total)

5 mins warm-up, then on a 350m hill, run 20 hills at 80–90% MHR. Jog down to recover between each. 5 mins cool-down to finish.

REST

LONG SLOW DISTANCE RUN
6 hours   *Constant pace (60% MHR)*

LONG SLOW DISTANCE RUN
5 hours   *Constant pace (60% MHR)*

REST

INTERVAL TRAINING
10 x 1,000m intervals

Intervals at 80% MHR with 200m jog between intervals.

REST

HILL TRAINING
90 mins (total)

5 mins warm-up, then on a 350m hill, run 20 hills at 80–90% MHR. Jog down to recover between each. 5 mins cool-down to finish.

REST

LONG SLOW DISTANCE RUN
6 hours   *Constant pace (60% MHR)*

LONG SLOW DISTANCE RUN
6 hours   *Constant pace (60% MHR)*

To stay injury-free, try to vary the surface you run on to reduce the impact on your joints.

	29	30
MONDAY	REST	REST
TUESDAY	**INTERVAL TRAINING** **10 x 1,000m intervals** *Intervals at 80% MHR with 200m jog between intervals.*	**STEADY RUN** **90 mins** *Constant easy pace (60% MHR)*
WEDNESDAY	REST	REST
THURSDAY	**HILL TRAINING** **90 mins (total)** *5 mins warm-up, then on a 350m hill, run 20 hills at 80–90% MHR. Jog down to recover between each. 5 mins cool-down to finish.*	**STEADY RUN** Getting time on your feet. Run at a pace you can still chat. **90 mins** *Constant easy pace (60% MHR)*
FRIDAY	REST	REST
SATURDAY	**LONG SLOW DISTANCE RUN** **7 hours** *Constant pace (60% MHR)*	**LONG SLOW DISTANCE RUN** **4 hours** *Constant pace (60% MHR)*
SUNDAY	**LONG SLOW DISTANCE RUN** **6 hours** *Constant pace (60% MHR)*	**LONG SLOW DISTANCE RUN** **2 hours** *Constant pace (60% MHR)*

REST

REST

STEADY RUN
Run at a relaxed pace.

50 mins   *Constant easy pace (60% MHR)*

STEADY RUN
This warm-up run should feel easy and enjoyable.

30 mins   *Constant easy pace (60% MHR)*

REST

REST

STEADY RUN
Get time on your feet with this gentle jog.

50 mins   *Constant easy pace (60% MHR)*

EASY RUN
Stretch your legs out and take it easy.

30 mins   *Constant easy pace (60% MHR)*

REST

REST

LONG SLOW DISTANCE RUN

2 hours   *Constant pace (60% MHR)*

REST

LONG SLOW DISTANCE RUN

2 hours   *Constant pace (60% MHR)*

RACE DAY
You've made it, now it's just your ultra distance event to go. Enjoy it. You've worked hard!

THE TRACK

TRACK SESSIONS

At certain points during your training you will need to inject some variations in speed work, as well as drills that will help you improve strength to create the technique necessary for maximum performance, stability and efficiency of movement.

A 400-metre track is the perfect place to accurately assess performance and gives you a flat, consistent surface for drills and speed work in particular. The following track-based programmes are the sort of thing that top-class runners use in their training all of the time and form a bedrock of stamina and endurance development, which will change your ability to cope with long runs in future.

Follow the track sessions as prescribed in the programmes and keep an accurate measure of your performance in each of them. Measuring your "split" times for each 400-metre circuit or kilometre lets you fine-tune your training and gives you focus to improve every time.

Track sessions are one of the easiest things to avoid, either because there isn't a track close to you or just because you don't have the inclination to try a different approach to your running. It is understandable that you should have reservations and you might feel as though you just don't fit in at a track where people are performing at a high level. However, just like the gym, nobody is really watching you (I promise), so focus on yourself and don't worry about it. If getting to a track really is difficult for you, try to measure out a distance in your park that is the same size and use that as your training base instead.

In some ways these sessions are the hardest but best type of training. They can feel like the worst because they are very challenging – you will find that you push yourself to achieve certain times for key distances and your legs *will* feel it. However, completing these highly structured programmes will leave you with the greatest sense of personal satisfaction and will rapidly improve your running performance elsewhere.

There are 5 main track-based sessions that you should, and will, be building into your running training. Before each of the sessions you should follow the procedures of warm-up stretches and mobility drills as detailed on pages 52–61.

1. FARTLEK TRAINING

This is one of the most commonly used and successful forms of track training for middle- and long-distance athletes and is based upon Scandinavian principles of training, with the word itself stemming from the Scandinavian term for "speed play".

Within each fartlek session you alter your speed between low, medium and fast pace, and repeat this pattern throughout the session's duration (unless you are opting for the random speed changes session detailed below). There are three alternative routines you can follow:

Jog slowly for 100m.
Run 200m at a medium to fast pace.
Run 100m at a fast pace.
This completes 1 lap of a 400m track. Repeat this pattern for 10–15 laps depending on fitness levels.

Jog slowly for 75m.
Run 75m at a medium to fast pace.
Run 50m at a fast pace.
You will do 2 complete cycles of this for each 400m lap. Repeat this pattern for 4–6 laps and then rest for 2 mins before repeating in the same pattern 2–3 times, depending on fitness levels.

Complete random speed changes with a partner.
Take turns to lead for 2 laps of a 400m track at a time, with the leader randomly changing speed for 50–100m long distances between low, medium and fast pace. This approach makes both parties think about testing the other out by pushing ahead, or by keeping up and keeping the pressure high. Repeat this pattern for 10–15 laps.

2. THRESHOLD RUNS

By raising the point at which your body produces large amounts of lactic acid you will enable yourself to run faster for further than you could before. Training needs to be carried out at a level that is quick and challenging so that your body is forced to adapt to a higher demand level. This in turn will reduce the chances of you needing to slow down during a run while trying to reach a new best time or complete a new distance. A flat track surface is perfect for this type of training as it allows a consistent level of overload for each high-intensity section and also allows you to measure the distance of each faster run and analyse the reduced performance over the session.

1. Run at a speed that is the equivalent to the speed you would run for a 3–5K run.
This should feel as though you are able to sustain pace only for a limited period of time before feeling some minor fatigue kick in.

2. Hold this pace for between three and five minutes.
Take a slow-pace jogging recovery period of between 90 secs and 3 mins until you feel as though the fatigue has partially subsided. Repeat the running time again for a total of 4–6 runs.

3. TEMPO RUNS

Holding your running pace at a level close to your anaerobic threshold level for extended periods is a great way to extend your endurance levels and increase your long-distance running pace. Maintain good form at all times during this session.

1. Run for 12–15 mins at a pace marginally faster than you would run for 10K.
Rest by jogging at a slow pace for 3 mins.

2. Run for 10–12 mins at a fast 5K running pace.
Rest by jogging slowly for 3 mins.

3. Run for 5 mins at a moderate to fast pace. Your muscles should fatigue at 2–3 mins.

4. MAXIMUM INTENSITY INTERVALS

This type of training is designed to really overload the heart, lungs, legs and mind as you push through some barriers and attain a higher level of fitness and speed endurance. Using a track is perfect for this training as it involves high speed and you will need to have distances accurately measured to define your targets for each run. There are two alternative programmes you can follow:

Run for 400m at a moderate to fast pace. You should experience muscular and cardiovascular fatigue at the end of each run.
Walk for 150m, then slowly jog for 150m.
Repeat pattern 5 times.

Run 400m at a moderate to fast pace.
Jog slowly for 100m.
Repeat pattern 10–12 times, or split into 2 sets of 5–6 runs with a 3-min rest between sets.

With both of these sessions you are required to put in a high level of effort for a period of time that is long enough to really challenge your ability. The rest period in both cases is relatively short and is a time of "active recovery" rather than total "stop".

5. STRIDING OUT

This approach is something that is used by sprinters to prepare for a race. It is a less intensive session than the others detailed here, but it is a very effective way of concentrating on good running technique and thinking about tension points in your torso, neck and shoulders, as well as your breathing pattern.

By repeatedly doing striding sessions you are able to focus on the fine detail of your technique and feel comfortable with your running. Sometimes the pressure of trying to work at a high rate all of the time can be tough, so a session that keeps your body moving without taking too much out of you can make for a nice change. You should feel some moderate workload during this session, in the legs and in the heart and lungs but you should not feel as though you reach full fatigue level at any point.

1. Stride out for 60–100m at 70–80% of your maximum running speed. Concentrate on perfecting your running technique as you do so.

2. Rest for 30–45 secs.
Repeat sequence for a total of 5 runs. Take a walking rest for 3 mins before repeating the pattern again for another 1–2 groups of 5 runs.

THE
EXERCISES

RESISTANCE TRAINING

Most runners just like to run. However, to really achieve the most from your body and, importantly, to greatly reduce your risk of injury, strength training is a vital facet to your running training.

Running requires a great deal of muscular strength, not only in the legs but also in the buttocks, hips, back, abdominals, and (to a lesser but important degree) the arms.

Strength provides propulsion, stability and helps to achieve greater levels of stamina and endurance as a result. The potential for improvement is greater within strength training than within cardiovascular training as your body has a lesser return from cardio training overall. Strength can be improved significantly and while there can be concerns from runners about gaining muscle mass and making the legs in particular feel "heavy", the gains that you will experience as a result of the extra strength are greater than any potential downside that extra muscle might bring. You should also note that the type and frequency of strength training that you will be carrying out is not aimed at making great gains in muscle size, and when combined with the high level of endurance training that the programmes require you to complete, the chances of gaining any significant muscle size are minimal.

The very nature of running is that you have one foot in contact with the ground at a time, therefore some of the drills and resistance programmes feature this approach to prepare the body for what it will actually go through while you run. It is stability and power that is required when the foot strikes, as your body has to control the enormous shift in workload from one side of the body to the other and in a diagonal plane across the body (as your left leg works, your right shoulder activates predominantly), which requires great strength through the middle of the body which must continue outwards from that point.

The combination of the drills in this book with these strength training plans produce a combined strengthening and mobilising effect that will help to maximise your performance. Don't duck these sessions; they will genuinely transform your running.

REPETITION MAXIMUM

Repetitions maximum or "RM" is the number of repetitions of an exercise that you should perform using a weight that allows you to complete that number of repetitions and no more. For example, if you are told to do 15 RM, by the end of the fifteenth repetition you should not be able to do another. Finding the correct weight for your RM in each exercise takes some practice but it is important because the exercise routines are designed to work with a specific technique and level of overload in mind.

RESISTANCE A1

Step-Up	*20 reps each leg*	**p185**
Single Leg Bodylift	*20 reps each leg*	**p179**
Russian Twist	*30 reps*	**p178**
Hyper Extension	*20 reps*	**p172**
Box Jump	*20 reps*	**p169**
Hamstring Curl	*20 reps*	**p172**
Knee Cross-Over Tuck	*30 reps each side*	**p173**
Hyper Extension	*20 reps*	**p172**
Single Leg Deadlift	*15 reps each leg*	**p180**

repeat this exercise circuit 2–4 times
rest for 1 min between circuits

RESISTANCE A2

Squat with Dumbbells	*20–30 reps*	**p183**
Dumbbell Press	*18–20 RM*	**p171**
Walking Lunge	*20–30 reps*	**p187**
Single Arm Row	*15 RM*	**p179**

repeat this exercise circuit 1–3 times depending on fitness levels
rest for 30 secs between circuits

Plank	*40–60 secs*	**p177**
Reverse Curl	*15–30 reps*	**p178**

complete 3–5 sets of each exercise, alternating between them
rest for 30 secs between sets

RESISTANCE B1

Single Leg Squat	*30/25/20 secs each leg*	**p182**
Tricep Dip	*45/40/35 secs*	**p186**
Burpee	*45/40/35 secs*	**p170**

rest for 45 secs between each sets and 60 secs between exercises

Step-Up	*30/25/20 secs*	**p185**
Bent-Over Row	*30/25/20 secs*	**p169**
Single Leg Hop-Over	*20/20/20 secs*	**p181**

rest for 30 secs between sets and 60 secs between exercises

Lateral Lunge	*40/35/30 secs*	**p174**
Plyometric Lunge	*40/30/20 secs*	**p177**
Step-to-Box Jump	*40/30/20 secs*	**p184**

rest for 30 secs between sets and 60 secs between exercises

RESISTANCE B2

Squat	*8/7/6/5/4 RM*	**p182**
Single Leg Deadlift	*8/7/6/5/4 RM*	**p180**
Lunge and Single Arm Raise	*40/40/30/30/20 reps*	**p174**

rest for 30 secs between sets and 60 secs between exercises

Walking Lunge with Rotation	*10 reps*	**p187**
Lateral Lunge	*20 reps*	**p174**
Squat Thrust	*20 reps*	**p183**

repeat this exercise circuit twice
rest for 1 min between circuits

Upright Row	*15 reps*	**p186**
Asymmetric Press-Up	*to failure*	**p168**
Russian Twist	*30 reps*	**p178**

repeat this exercise circuit twice
rest for 1 min between circuits

Dumbbell Rotation	*20 reps*	**p171**
Medicine Ball Reach-Up	*20 reps*	**p175**

repeat this exercise circuit twice
rest for 1 min between circuits

AB ROUTINES

A stronger core supports your spine and will enable you to run more effectively. Pick and complete one of these ab routines on the days that you have resistance training.

ROUTINE 1

Ab Crunch	*30 reps*	**p168**
Oblique Crunch	*30 reps*	**p175**
Plank	*40 secs*	**p177**
Oblique Plank	*40 secs*	**p176**

repeat each exercise in turn, and repeat whole routine 2–5 times

ROUTINE 2

Single Leg Reverse Curl	*30 reps*	**p181**
Oblique Plank Raise	*15 reps*	**p176**
Single Leg Bridge	*15 secs*	**p180**
Knee Cross-Over Tuck	*30 reps*	**p173**
Hyper Extension	*25 secs*	**p172**

repeat each exercise in turn, and repeat whole routine 2–5 times

ROUTINE 3

Single Leg Bodylift	*15 reps*	**p179**
Standing Abductor Raise	*20 reps*	**p184**
Single Leg Squat	*12 reps*	**p182**
Clam	*25 secs*	**p170**
Straight Leg Donkey Kick	*25 secs*	**p185**

repeat each exercise in turn, and repeat whole routine 2–5 times

Ab Crunch

An exercise that targets the upper portion of the abdominal muscles. If performed properly, it helps develop abdominal strength.

1 Lie on your back with your feet flat to the floor, tighten the abdominals and place your hands by your ears.

2 Curl your upper body forward while ensuring that the lower back does not lift from the floor, keeping the chin tucked toward the chest throughout the movement. Once the shoulders are lifted from the floor, lower slowly back down. Repeat for the set number of repetitions.

Asymmetric Press-Up

A twist on the regular press-up, this isolates each side of the upper body in turn.

1 Assume a standard press-up position, face down but with one hand on the floor and the other on a low box or step. Both hands should be directly under the shoulders and your legs extended with the balls of your feet touching the ground. Now bend your elbows, keeping your shoulders parallel to the ground.

2 Lower your torso to the ground until your elbows form an approximate 90° angle, before raising yourself back up by attempting to push the ground away from you. Repeat for the other side.

Bent-Over Row

The bent-over row is a multi-joint movement that's great for stimulating strengthening the posterior muscles of the back.

1 Holding a barbell or dumbbells in a wide position, bend your body from the hips, keeping your lower back straight.

2 Pull the bar towards the base of your chest, keeping the elbows in a wide position and pulling your shoulder blades close together. Return to the start position and repeat for the set number of repetitions.

Box Jump

This is an excellent exercise for developing explosive strength in the legs as it requires you to develop your jumping force from a dead stop.

1 Assume a deep squat position in front of a medium-sized box with your hands by your hips.

2 Jump up with both feet onto the box, trying to keep your back straight as you do so.

3 Land softly in a squat position on the balls of your feet. Step backwards to the starting position and repeat for the set number of repetitions.

Burpee

A full-body exercise that hits legs, abs and upper body all in one dynamic movement. This exercise is the ultimate bodyweight pulse-raiser.

1 Begin with your hands touching the floor and your knees tucked tight into the body.

2 Kick your feet straight back out behind you before bringing them back in again to the starting position.

3 Come into a standing position by leaping up in the air with both arms raised. Return again to the starting position and repeat.

Clam

This simple exercise tones the hips and thighs and teaches pelvic stability as the leg rotates inward and outward at the hip.

1 Lie on your side with your hips and shoulders in a straight line. Bend your knees so that your thighs are at 90° to your body. Rest your head on your top arm and stack your legs slightly apart.

2 Keeping the insides of the feet touching at all times, slowly open up your legs by engaging the glute of the upper leg. Lower down slowly until your knees meet. Repeat as necessary.

Dumbbell Press

Challenge shoulder stability with this dumbbell variant of the barbell or "chest" press. The shoulder stabilisers have to work harder to stabilise the arm as you perform the movement.

1 Holding dumbbells, lie back on a bench with your palms facing down towards your feet. Hold your arms straight out above you.

2 Lower the weight towards your chest, bending at the elbows until they are at a 90° angle to the chest. Push the weights straight back up to the starting position and repeat for the desired number of reps.

Dumbbell Rotation

A great exercise for building strength in the core.

1 Start by holding a dumbbell in front of you. Squat down, making sure you push your hips back and keep your back straight.

2 Pivot and rotate your hips to your right, keeping your back straight. Return to the centre before repeating in the opposite direction.

Hamstring Curl

Target the back of the legs in this exercise that works one of the areas of the body which stores stubborn body fat.

1 Lie down with your back against a mat and heels resting on a Swiss ball. Press your heels into the ball and raise your hips off the mat until all your bodyweight is resting on the upper back and shoulders.

2 Hold this position and roll the ball towards yourself by bending your legs back and pulling the ball in with the heels. Push the ball away by straightening the legs to return to the starting position. Repeat for the desired number of repetitions.

Hyper Extension

An exercise that targets the extension of the thoracic area of the back which commonly becomes hunched due to poor posture.

1 Start by lying on your front on the mat. Make sure you keep a straight line throughout your body from ankles, knees, hips, shoulders and neck.

2 Lift your chest off the floor, making sure your chin is tucked in. Hold this top position for a few seconds and then lower under control. Repeat for the set number of reps.

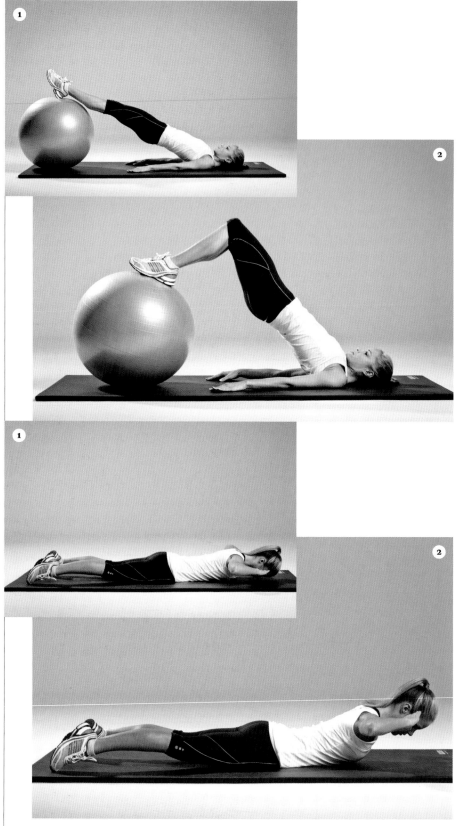

Knee Cross-Over Tuck

This basic abdominal exercise is great for developing stability around the lower back.

1 Assume a face-down position on the ground with palms of hands on the floor under the shoulders and legs extended with the balls of your feet touching the ground. Raise yourself up using your arms, maintaining a stable, straight torso.

2 Holding this position, slowly lift one foot off the floor and raise the leg, bringing the knee towards and across the upper body. Stop raising the leg at the point you feel your lower back bending and slowly lower back down to the starting position. Repeat on the other side.

Knee Tuck

Target the lower abdominals with this core-control-based exercise.

1 Assume a face-down position on the ground with palms of hands on the floor under the shoulders and legs extended with the balls of your feet touching the ground. Raise yourself up using your arms, maintaining a stable, straight torso.

2 Holding this position, slowly lift one foot off the floor and raise the leg, bringing the knee towards the upper body. Stop raising the leg at the point you feel your lower back bending and slowly lower back down to the starting position. Repeat on the other side.

Lateral Lunge

A great mobility exercise for the hip area which also challenges single leg balance. The lateral nature of this movement means that, compared to traditional movements of forwards and backwards, there is an element of stabilising against lateral forces.

1 Start in a standing position with good posture and tense your core muscles.

2 Step to the right bending the right knee to 90° while maintaining a straight left leg and torso. Push straight back up, taking a step back to the middle, and repeat to the other side. For added intensity add a weighted ball, barbell or dumbbells.

Lunge and Single Arm Raise

A lower-body mobility exercise combined with a single arm movement to enhance mobility in the upper-back area.

1 Lunge forward, engaging your core to maintain good posture.

2 As you ascend, raise your opposite arm upwards. So if you step forward with your left leg, you raise your right arm upwards. Complete the set number of reps before repeating on the other side.

Medicine Ball Reach-Up

This abdominal exercise forces you to control your core muscles. The added resistance makes it particularly effective.

1 Holding a medicine ball in both hands at your chest, lie on your back and lift your legs up so they are 90° to the floor.

2 Holding the medicine ball, reach upwards towards the end of your toes. Hold this position for a second before relaxing back into the starting position. Repeat for the set number of repetitions.

Oblique Crunch

This exercise is a bit of an old classic. Think of contracting the love handles as you twist across – and don't give up; it's only a bit of pain!

1 Lie on your back with your feet close to your buttocks and your hands by your ears.

2 Keeping your hands by your ears, twist your body so that you are aiming to reach your right elbow to your left knee. Repeat on the other side and for the set number of reps.

Oblique Plank

This stability drill enhances shoulder and abdominal strength. A good, strong abdominal area helps you with all your other exercises.

1 Lie on your side and elevate your body supporting your weight between your forearm and feet. Keep your body straight with the hips off the floor; the neck and back should stay straight. Hold this position for as long as required. Repeat on the other side.

Oblique Plank Raise

Challenge the oblique muscles with this lateral, flexion-based exercise.

1 Lie on your side and elevate your body, supporting your weight between your forearm and feet. Keep your body straight with your hips off the floor; your neck and back should stay straight.

2 Lower your hip towards the floor without touching and then raise yourself back up again. Repeat for the set number of repetitions.

Plank

The main test of core strength in this abdominal-bracing drill challenges the static strength of the abdominals. Stronger abs means a greater ability to prevent injury, which from a training perspective will help deliver better, longer-lasting results.

1 Lie face down on a mat with your elbows on the ground and your arms out to your sides.

2 Elevate your body, keeping your weight distributed between your forearms and feet. Your elbows should be bent at a 90° angle. Keep your back straight with the hips raised off the floor. Squeeze the torso tight, ensuring the body is parallel to the floor. Hold this position for as long as required.

Plyometric Lunge

Plyometric lunges target the muscles of the leg which provide speed and endurance and differ from regular lunges because of the powerful, rapid movement involved.

1 Standing with your feet shoulder-width apart, step forward about one stride. Now lower your body down until your front thigh is parallel to the ground and your back knee is almost touching the ground.

2 As soon as you reach this point, explode back up and alternate leg positions in the air.

3 As you land, drop back down into the lunge before quickly repeating. Repeat for the set number of repetitions.

Reverse Curl

This exercise works the lower portion of the abdominal muscles, an area that is particularly important for general stability and injury prevention.

1 Lie on the floor on your back. Put your hands by your sides with your feet up and your thighs perpendicular to the floor. They should not go lower than this during the movement.

2 Using your lower abs, roll your pelvis to lower your hips towards the floor. Your legs will now be at a 45° angle to the floor. Return slowly to the starting position.

Russian Twist

This exercise is great for building strength in the abs as well as the muscles of your back and the obliques, as well as improving balance and flexibility.

1 Sit on the ground with your knees bent and your heels flat on the floor. Lean slightly back without rounding your spine at all until your knees are parallel with your chest. Keeping your hips as still as possible, rotate your shoulders so your upper body twists to the right.

2 Moving your whole torso, not just your arms, change shoulders and twist to the left. Repeat for the set number of repetitions. For added intensity add a weighted ball.

Single Arm Row
A single arm pulling exercise that helps develop shoulder retraction and balances against poor posture. This pulling exercise maintains the balance between push and pull – essential for maintaining a balanced posture and physique.

1 Kneeling on a bench with a flat back, hold one arm straight down level with the shoulder.

2 Lift the weight upwards until it is level with the back, squeezing the shoulder blades as you do so. Lower the weight back to the starting position to complete one repetition.

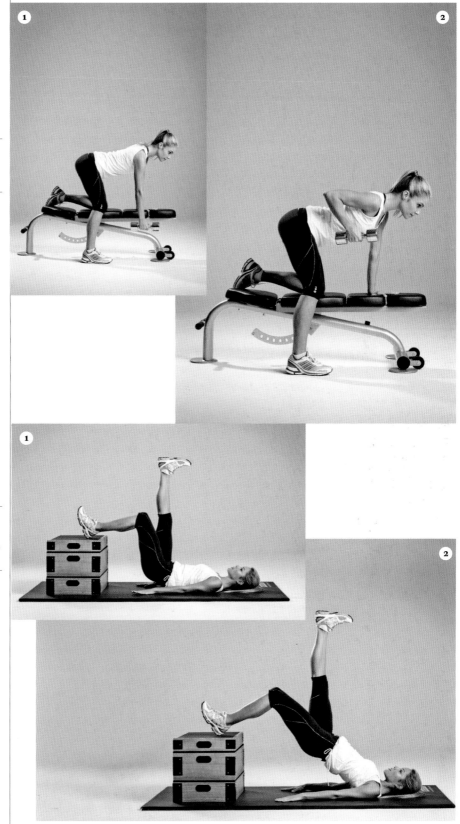

Single Leg Bodylift
The single leg version of the bodylift adds the additional challenge of rotational stability as you try to support your body on one leg.

1 Lie on your back with your feet on a bench or step. Remove one foot and point this upwards, at 90° to the floor.

2 Slowly lift your pelvis off the floor until your hips are in line with your shoulders. Slowly lower down into the starting position and repeat for the set number of repetitions.

Single Leg Bridge

This variation on the regular bridge places greater workload onto one side and will increase the feeling of overload quickly.

1 Lie on your back with your feet on the floor and your knees bent. Keep rolling your pelvis forwards and backwards until you are happy that you can find the mid-point (neutral pelvis). Hold this position. Remove one foot and hold this leg in line with the other leg.

2 Slowly lift your pelvis off the floor until your hips and knees are in line with your shoulders; make sure you keep both legs parallel. Slowly lower down into the starting position and repeat.

Single Leg Deadlift

The ultimate single leg exercise to challenge the glutes, hamstrings and the abdominal region. This exercise focuses on hip extension which is vital for developing a strong, lean and powerful physique.

1 Start by standing on one leg; engage your core to maintain good stability and posture.

2 Lean forward while maintaining a straight back, level hips and a slightly flexed knee – so you move from the hips as if hinged. Lower, maintaining this position and keeping the arm straight. Return to the starting position, squeezing the buttock muscles as you do so.

Single Leg Hop-Over
Target the lower leg with this hopping drill to improve reactive strength and stability.

1 Standing with your feet shoulder-width apart, and with your left leg raised so that your knee is parallel to your hips, lower yourself into a single leg squat.

2 Pushing up of your right leg, jump as far sideways as possible. Try to keep the body vertical and straight as you do so.

3 Land on the ball of your foot, anticipating the landing and springing up into the next repetition as quickly as you can.

Single Leg Reverse Curl
This exercise pushes the lower abdominals hard – an area that is typically weak in a lot of my trainees who have not been training hard enough!

1 Lie on your back with your knees pulled up at a 90° angle. Make sure you draw in your belly button towards the mat so that your lower back is in contact with the ground.

2 Extend your right leg straight out and then repeat with the other leg. Your heel should not touch the ground. Keep the abs tight throughout the movement. Repeat for the set number of repetitions.

Single Leg Squat

This is one of the most intensive leg exercises you can do and is a very effective way of strengthening the stabilising muscles of the inner and outer thigh.

1 Stand with your feet hip-width apart next to a knee-high bench or box. With your arms out in front of you and keeping your right leg straight, raise your left leg so that your knee is parallel to your hips.

2 Keeping your back straight, slowly lower your body until your buttocks are just above the box. Pause for 1 second, then push yourself up to return to the start position.

Squat

The king of lower body strength exercises, targeting the front of the thighs and the hips. This is one of the primary exercises that all trainees should be utilising in their training programmes.

1 Start in a standing position with your feet a little over shoulder-width apart and your arms crossed with your hands resting on your shoulders.

2 Bend from the hips, keeping your weight in your heels and maintaining a straight back, until your knees are at a 90° angle. Keeping your arms crossed, push back up to the start position without bending your back. Repeat for the set number of repetitions.

Squat with Dumbbells
A more intense version of the bodyweight squat with added load to increase the difficulty. The added weight provides more of a challenge to keep the body upright, therefore meaning more work for the abs.

1 Stand with your feet shoulder-width apart with your toes and knees slightly pointing outward. Hold dumbbells in your hands with your arms at your sides. Keep your back straight and your head up.

2 Squat down until your thighs are parallel to the floor. Slowly return to the starting position. Repeat for the set number of repetitions.

Squat Thrust
A hip-flexion-based exercise that increases lower body dynamism and takes your heart rate "through the roof".

1 Put your hands on the floor, shoulder-width apart, with your legs stretched out straight behind you.

2 Jump both legs towards your chest as far as you can by bending them at the knees. Return your legs to the starting position and repeat the exercise for the set number of repetitions.

Standing Abductor Raise

This exercise targets the muscles of the outer buttocks, the gluteus medius or hip abductor, and is also very effective at toning the outer thighs.

1 Hold onto a chair/exercise bench for balance and start with your your feet hip-width apart.

2 Lift your leg straight to the side about 30–45° with a slow and controlled movement. Take care not to lift your leg higher than 45° or to bend sideways at the waist. Hold for 1 second, then return to the start position.

Step-to-Box Jump

This exercise is an effective way of developing power in the leg muscles and increasing vertical jump height. When the box height is no longer challenging, jump onto a higher box.

1 Stand with your feet shoulder-width apart and one foot on top of a medium-sized box.

2 Jump up onto the box, trying to keep your body vertical with your arms raised as you do so. Step off the box to return to the starting position and repeat as necessary.

Step-Up

A movement that enhances hip extension, working through the glutes and hamstrings. Performed quickly, it can also be a very effective dynamic power-building exercise.

1 Stand straight with one foot on a bench and one on the floor.

2 Step up with one leg and follow with the other. Return to the starting position. Complete the set number of reps before repeating on the opposite side. For added intensity, add dumbbells or a barbell.

Straight Leg Donkey Kick

Working your glutes provides great strength and stability in the hips. This simple isolation exercise is an effective way of targeting the outer range of the hip movement, which is essential for good running posture and strength.

1 Face the floor with your knees and forearms supporting your body and your back straight. Straighten your right leg out behind you, keeping your left leg bent at 90°.

2 Keeping your right leg straight, lift it up toward the ceiling. Return to start position and repeat with your left leg.

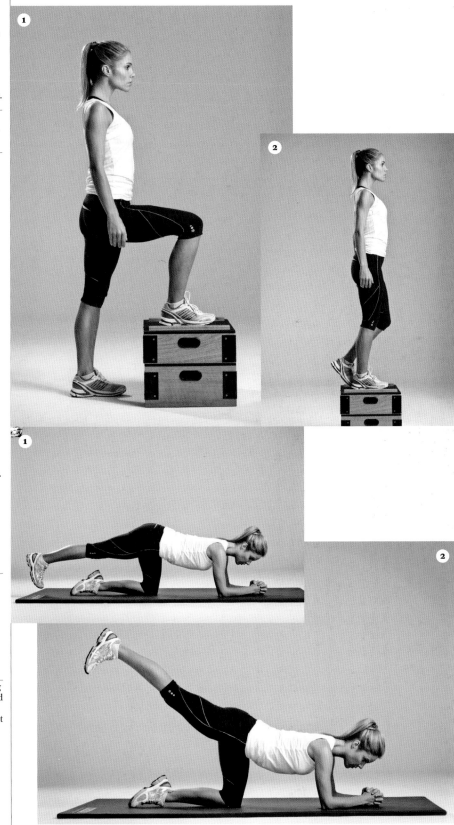

Tricep Dip

This highly effective exercise concentrates work on the triceps. Exercises that involve lifting your own bodyweight help to improve posture and strengthen and protect the skeletal system.

1 Position yourself in front of an exercise bench, with your palms on the bench facing forward and with your legs out in front of you.

2 Keeping your back straight, slowly lower yourself until your upper arms are bent at 90°. Hold this lower position for a moment before pushing back up until your arms are straight, but not locked.

Upright Row

Performed to a mid-chest level, this exercise targets the shoulders and the biceps. Be careful of lifting too heavy a weight, as this exercise can stress the shoulder muscles if not performed with correct technique.

1 Stand upright with your feet shoulder-width apart, holding a barbell or a pair of dumbbells in each hand.

2 Lift the barbell up to the top of your chest level, flexing your elbows until they are level with your jaw line. Return to the starting position to complete one repetition.

Walking Lunge

This is a great, dynamic exercise that hits all of the lower body muscles. An extension in intensity over the regular lunge, it takes balance, control and concentration.

1 Stand with your feet shoulder-width apart. Raise your left leg to hip level, bending your knee to 90°.

2 Step forwards into a lunge, bending both knees to 90°, before continuing straight into a standing position. Carry on your forward momentum, and repeat with the right leg. Repeat for the set number of repetitions.

Walking Lunge with Rotation

This dynamic lunge combined with a rotation-based abdominal movement will challenge your stability; the added rotation means that you have to maintain balance at the hip to stop yourself from falling over.

1 Stand with your feet about hip-width apart; take hold of the medicine ball with both hands in front of your chest. Take a step forward with one leg and plant the foot firmly down; the knees should be bent at 90° while the back remains upright.

2 In the lunge position, rotate the body to the side of the lunged leg, then back again. Drive the leg back to the start position. Repeat on the other leg.

GLOSSARY

AEROBIC CAPACITY
The body's ability to take in and utilise oxygen in the body. Aerobic exercise increases aerobic capacity.

AEROBIC EXERCISE
Exercise "with oxygen"; it builds heart and lung strength and enhances the body's ability to take in oxygen, feed oxygenated blood around the body and create energy. The long-term effects of aerobic exercise are lower blood pressure, decreased risk of heart problems and better circulation.

ABS/ABDOMINALS
These are the muscles of the stomach area. The muscle group extends from the rib cage to the pelvis and comprises three main muscles of importance: the rectus abdominus (the "six pack" muscles that run down the middle of the stomach), the obliques (the muscles on the outside of the stomach area) and the quadratus lumborum (the deep muscle that wraps around the mid-section of the torso and is important for posture).

ANAEROBIC EXERCISE
Exercise "without oxygen"; fast explosive work that cannot be sustained for long periods of time. This form of exercise uses the less efficient anaerobic energy system that can be maintained for only short bursts.

BICEPS
The muscles at the front of the upper arms; used to bend the arms.

CADENCE
The number of strides taken in a prescribed period of time.

FARTLEK TRAINING
A form of unstructured interval training, most suitable for outdoors, using a number of speed "bursts" which vary in number, duration and frequency.

FAST-TWITCH MUSCLES
These contract faster and more explosively than slow-twitch muscles (see opposite), are white in colour, have less resistance to fatigue and are used for anaerobic exercise. Sprinters and sportsmen who need short bursts of speed develop a greater proportion of fast-twitch muscles.

FOOT STRIKE
The point at which the foot hits the ground while running.

GLYCOGEN
A complex carbohydrate used as fuel for the muscles, obtained from eating starchy foods. A distance runner's best source of energy.

GLUTES
The muscles of the bottom and hip area, which are used in the action of moving the leg backwards.

HAMSTRINGS
The muscles at the backs of the thighs; used to bend the legs.

HIP FLEXOR
The muscles of the hip area; they are used in the action of bringing the knee up to the chest or raising the knee.

INTERVAL TRAINING
Carefully calculated periods of high-intensity exercise alternated with resting "recovery" periods designed to build cardiovascular endurance.

LACTIC ACID
A metabolic by-product of burning glycogen to power the muscles.

LATS/LATISSIMUS DORSI
The large muscle of the back, which is used in all actions pulling down and towards the body.

MAXIMUM HEART RATE (MHR)
The maximum level to which a person should raise their heart rate; it is determined by age and calculated in beats per minute (bpm).

PECS/PECTORALS
The muscles of the chest area, used in moving the arms forwards and pushing away from the body.

PRONATION
The degree your foot rolls inwards as you go through your running motion.

QUADS/QUADRICEPS
The muscles of the fronts of the thighs, used to straighten the legs.

REPETITION (REP)
In resistance training a rep is one complete performance of an exercise, moving from the start position to the end position. If you are asked to do 10 reps of an exercise, you should repeat that exercise 10 times before stopping.

REPETITION MAXIMUM (RM)
The number of repetitions of a particular exercise to be performed to achieve overload in the muscles.

RESISTANCE TRAINING
A training method that uses weights to tone and build the muscles.

SET
The number of repetitions you perform of an exercise in one go, without pausing, You are often asked to repeat sets, in which case you can take a short rest period between each set.

SPLIT
Splitting a course or a run into several different distance points – miles or kilometres, for instance – and recording your times for each section separately.

SLOW-TWITCH MUSCLES
These muscle fibres have a slower contraction time and are capable of storing more oxygen than fast-twitch fibres.

TEMPO TRAINING
A generic term used to describe a steady state run of moderate to long distance that's performed at a moderate to moderately hard pace. Tempo runs are designed to get the body to work at anaerobic threshold level – the level at which anaerobic energy paths start to operate – and will in time improve the duration at which you can hold a good pace.

INDEX

ACKNOWLEDGEMENTS

Thank you to everyone who contributed to making this book, as always it is a team effort that has produced a brilliant piece of work.

Thank you first to the members of my team who were involved in a range of ways. Jon, Sally, Ian, Ayo and Luke all contributed text, time or body to the cause!

Thank you to all at Quadrille, in particular Simon, Anne, Helen, Claire and Mark for their hard work on all aspects of the book.

Thank you again to Chris Terry for the excellent shots – they look really terrific – and to our model, Lyndsay.

And, of course, I want to mention my family, particularly my daughter Amber who at 8 years old has already raced in 5K events, and my son Ben, who doesn't seem to stop running. You're never too young to start!

Editorial Director Anne Furniss
Creative Director Helen Lewis
Project Editor Simon Davis
Designer Claire Peters
Photographer Chris Terry
Production Director Vincent Smith
Production Controller James Finan
Hair and Make-Up Maria Comparetto
Models Lindsay Jay, Ayo Williams, Luke Weal

Picture Credits
p.127 © Getty Images
p.131 © Getty Images

First published in 2011 by
Quadrille Publishing Limited
Alhambra House
27–31 Charing Cross Road
London WC2H 0LS
www.quadrille.co.uk

Text © 2011 Matt Roberts
Photography © 2011 Chris Terry
Design and layout © 2011 Quadrille Publishing Ltd

Cataloguing in Publication Data: a catalogue record for this book is available from the British Library.

ISBN 978 184949 083 2

Printed in China